Love from
Diana

Love from
Diana

Diana, *Queen of Hearts*
& Michael Joseph

Magus

"She was the Queen of the world."

Florence Mdaka

Republic of South Africa
September, 1997

This edition printed in 2005 by Magus
An imprint of Arcturus Publishing Limited
26/27 Bickels Yard, 151–153 Bermondsey Street
London SE1 3HA

ISBN 1-84193-345-7

Printed in UK

Set in Perpetua
Typeset by Mike Harrington MATS, Southend-on-Sea, Essex
& Arcturus Publishing Limited

Author's note

I HAVE NO MONOPOLY on truth — I have only my own truth to tell. What we are attempting here is simply to urge you to seek yours; to share some vital information with you that might help you to make the most of your own personal journey or mission or quest. And to encourage you to look forward to your next one!

Love from
Diana

I am well aware that a lot of people — many of them publishers! — don't believe in an 'afterlife' or 'higher worlds', and don't trust communications that purport to come from them. Some of the reviewers of this book will almost certainly think along those lines.

I have every sympathy with them: until 1966, I was a fully paid-up member of their ranks, and regarded 'mediumship' as just so much vapourware. Then something happened that changed my mind — and my life — forever. Someone I loved, who had died suddenly at the age of 36, at the height of her powers — England's much-loved pop singer, Alma Cogan — tapped me on the shoulder and whispered intimacies that only she and I could possibly have known about. At that moment, the doors to the next Universe swung open — and have remained open ever since.

More often than not, my friends and loved ones in that next Universe come to me directly, not through any intermediary, when they have something to tell me, or to give me, or to ask. And that, as you'll see, is how this book came into existence.

M.J.

"During her brief sojourn in the physical world, Diana showed us just how much one person's love, compassion, real courage and fighting spirit can accomplish.

Now this astonishing book reveals her true majesty and higher purpose. She possesses the rare ability to reach us *all* . . . Her words are perfectly timed to encourage and inspire us as we step into the new Millennium."

Peter Quiller
Author of Merlin Awakens *and* Quest For The Round Table (*Dragonfly*)

"A wonderful evocation of Diana – past, present and future – certainly unique in its content and assembly; and while others have dwelt on her human character and frailties, you reveal her spiritual purpose. Perfect that they should both appear on the stage at the same moment, as together they form the official record of her life in all its many and varied aspects."

Simon Peter Fuller
Wholistic World Vision

Contents

— Contents —

Diana speaks!

5 February, 2003

Now that a few years have elapsed since my 'death', so-called, I have been invited to say my piece. An invitation I am more than happy to accept.

When I look back at my recent life on Earth, I have very few regrets – and all of them are related to my own weaknesses, to the many opportunities I missed. I have no scores to settle, no axes to grind – maybe just a few apologies to make!

The main purpose of this book is to share some wonderful news with you. And as I'm speaking these words myself, I think you can guess what that news is.

Yes, 'death' is an illusion. It's only the end of a chapter in our lives: for every one of us, the story goes on. I'm back where I came from – where we *all* come from.

And talking of the end of a chapter, you've doubtless noticed the dramatic changes that are occurring every day at almost unbelievable speed. Welcome them, even though some of them are rather unnerving, because they mark the end of this particular age, with all its pain and cruelty and injustice.

The coming age is going be something else altogether. So tear up the old rulebook, and write a new one. Create your *own* future, your *own* destiny – for heaven's sake, don't let anyone else do it for you!

Love from
Diana

Introduction

*In this quarter century, your dream produces
its harvest. The bridge between
Creator and Creation appears . . .*

Ken Carey
Starseed: The Third Millennium
1991

IT HAPPENS THAT I have encouraged quite a number of people to write books in my day, but this is the first time I have ever helped someone in another dimension to do so.

One example of the former, if I may.

For more than thirty years, publishers on both sides of the Atlantic begged the celebrated film star Ava Gardner to write her memoirs, but she always refused. She was a friend of mine for sixteen years, and finally I told her she had to.

"All the other books about you are scissors-and-paste jobs by lazy journalists who just look up old press files on your fist-fights with Sinatra, or your affairs with bullfighters. But only *you* know how it was during Hollywood's glory years."

"But I'm not a writer, honey," she would always protest.

"You don't have to be," I argued. "All you need is a glass of wine, a pack of cigarettes, a cassette recorder and – this is very important – a list of chapter headings, so you can choose which subject to tackle each day. It doesn't have to be done in sequence – your editor will stitch it all together."

She still looked highly doubtful.

"Listen, you were *there!* " I persisted. "You've got such an amazing overview of all the Hollywood glamour and bullshit and excess, *and* your own inimitable tone of voice, *and* sense of humour, which no-one else could ever recreate. So *go* for it."

When she died, a few years later, they found 90 tapes in her Knightsbridge apartment.

Result? *AVA: My Story*, edited and published by Bantam, which rocketed into the *New York Times* best-seller list and stayed there for weeks.

"Ava remains in a class by herself," declared Liz Smith in *The Daily News*. "This is one film star who lived up to her legend."

"Blunt and beautiful as the dame herself," pronounced *The Philadelphia Enquirer*. "This, her farewell appearance, is one of her best."

But now back to the present.

I have to admit that, ever since she left us, I've been urging Diana to build a bridge between this world and the next, by writing about her new life and telling us about some of the things we *all* have to look forward to, when our lives down here are over. But I never imagined that she'd ask *me* to help her with it.

Early one October morning, I was awoken by a familiar voice that whispered, "Okay, Michael, it's time to boot up, we've got work to do."

Heart pounding, I jumped out of bed and did as requested – and this is the result.

To this day, I'm not quite sure why I was selected for the job. Maybe the solution to the mystery lies in the next few pages.

You be the judge.

Just before you begin, a rather remarkable coincidence has just occurred to me. Many years ago my late uncle, the publisher Michael Joseph, also persuaded a very famous woman who had been denied the title 'Her Royal Highness' to write a book.

He had several meetings with the Duke and Duchess of Windsor at their home in Paris, and persuaded them, despite their initial reluctance, that the much-maligned 'Mrs Simpson' had every right to offer the world her own side of the story, and to record her innermost thoughts and feelings about the Abdication crisis that their relationship had precipitated.

The result of these meetings was her book *The Heart Has Its Reasons*.

Michael Joseph

i

Awesome Welles (i)

Back IN 1963 (can it *really* be half a lifetime ago?) the Italian film producer Dino de Laurentiis decided to film the Bible – or parts of it, at least. He asked four of the world's most eminent directors to prepare a script. One of them was Orson Welles.

In the spring of 1964, Orson came to London to cast his segment of the picture. My good friend Ronan O'Rahilly, whom I had been helping to launch the offshore music station *Radio Caroline*, urged me to see the great man, so we had a simple white linen costume made, and took some photographs by a lake at Virginia Water, just outside London. One of them turned out just right, so we were armed and ready.

The day came, and I was ushered into a third-floor office on the north side of Golden Square in Soho. There, behind a desk, was the legend himself, relaxed and smiling, Havana cigar on the go. Beside him sat his English casting director, Bill Chappell.

Maybe because he was so genial and informal and utterly lacking self-importance, I immediately felt at ease in the presence of someone who might have stepped down off Mount Olympus – and probably did – to show us mere mortals how to play with our new toy, motion pictures.

I handed the photo to Orson. The famous left eyebrow rose. He showed it to Chappell, then returned his gaze to me. "Are you an actor?"

"I used to run my own studio," I replied, "training actors for work in front of cameras."

"Even better!" bellowed Orson, removing the cigar and roaring with laughter. He studied the photograph again, nodded, reached a decision.

He glanced at Chappell.

"We've found our young Jacob," he announced.

Then he leaned forward to take my outstretched hand, and indicated the photo. "I'll show this to Dino De Laurentiis in Rome, and we'll be in touch."

I thanked him and Bill Chappell and rejoined Ronan in reception.

A few days later it was announced that, instead of an eight-hour extravaganza, the film would, after all, be of conventional length. Orson and two of the other directors were no longer attached to the picture; John Huston, who was to concentrate on the story of Noah — and play him, too — would direct.

My dream of working with Orson burst like a bubble.

ii

The Lady

Iℕ 1966 I was summoned by a friend to meet a man who told me there were certain things I should know, and offered to instruct me, if I wished him to. Flattered and mystified, I agreed – and he became my teacher.

In the late summer of the next year – that unforgettable year, which was crowned by the Beatles' *Sergeant Pepper* album – I was sitting alone with my instructor when he suddenly stopped speaking and gazed into the corner of the room behind me. After a moment he announced that "the Holy Lady" was approaching with a number of attendants.

I asked who she was.

"The feminine aspect of God; the instrument of the supreme Nature power; the intelligence of Nature that has been worshipped under different names throughout history," he replied.

I was stunned. I wondered why she was visiting us.

"She says she has reviewed your lives on the akashic record," my instructor went on, answering my unspoken question. "She's telling me you have unconsciously worshipped her throughout your lives, and you have spent much of your present life looking for an ideal woman."

I suddenly remembered that ever since I was a small boy, I had been trying to draw or paint a woman's face – an idealised face, perfect yet real; a face I already *knew* – but it always eluded me.

"She is saying that she is aware of what you are trying to achieve, and has now become your patron. But she will not allow your work to go out into the world until it is as perfect as can be. Should you ever need someone to help you revise or complete any project, she will see that they come to you. She gives you her blessing, and says she'll leave a sign of her visit. She is leaving now."

Rather shyly, I thanked her for her visit and for her help.

When she had gone, my instructor said that this was only the third time he had encountered the Lady. Then he smiled.

"Well, chum, you've got some friends in *very* high places. Don't let it go to your head."

That night I went home, undressed and got into bed.

A star was shining down on me out of the darkness.

I turned on the light and examined the ceiling closely.

A year before, I had stuck a number of luminous stars to the ceiling, but six months later my flat had been redecorated and the stars had all vanished beneath two layers of paint. But the paint had now been removed from the largest of these stars!

I got back into bed and stared at it for several minutes, remembering the Lady's visit, and her promise.

From out of the blue, with no warning whatsoever, a second major influence had come into my life. Until the Lady appeared, I was only half a person, unaware of the real importance of feminine energy and natural wisdom. But ever since that evening, I have tended to see history and the mounting catalogue of world crises from a woman's perspective rather than from a man's.

As every day passes I grow more and more convinced that 'the fall of Man' dates from the time when men stopped listening to women – if they ever did. The Adam and Eve story casts Eve as the 'heavy', but I reckon that's a disgraceful slander, designed to keep women in their place. The same was to happen to Mary Magdalene, Morgan le Fay, *and* several million wise-women/midwives in Europe during the Dark Ages. But that is another story which, one day, will surely be told.

iii

The Generals

Between 1967 and 1971, while my mentor and I were having our traditional Sunday evening conversations, he would occasionally look behind me and tell me I had another 'visitor'. They were almost always military men. During this period I was visited by Field Marshal Earl Alexander of Tunis, Field Marshal Slim, Lord Auchinleck, Lord Gort, Lord Wavell and several others.

By an odd coincidence, a dozen or so years earlier, while doing two weeks' Territorial Army service, I had had a brief personal encounter with Lord Alexander. My regiment was taking part in manoeuvres on Salisbury plain, and the infantry in the front lines had been instructed to dig in, in expectation of an atomic explosion that was due to go off at 15.00 hours that afternoon! My platoon was at the extreme right flank of the front line.

As digging proceeded – the trenches were no more than two or three feet deep – a distant dragonfly morphed into a camouflaged helicopter which landed nearby, and who should jump down but Field Marshal Alexander, followed by his adjutant.

I came to attention and saluted the great man.

"What are you doing?" he asked crisply, in that famous, no-nonsense manner of his.

With considerable effort, I kept a straight face.

"We're digging in, sir, as an atomic explosion is expected over there," – I indicated the skyline – "at 15.00 hours."

A fat lot of good trenches would be if a *real* nuclear explosion occurred, I was thinking. And so was Alexander, probably.

"Very well, carry on," he said.

Having descended from heaven to visit his humble foot-soldiers, the warrior demigod and his adjutant climbed back into their sky-chariot and floated away . . .

Mystified, I asked my mentor why these commanders were dropping in on us like this. His answer surprised me:

"You are a soldier. You have a soldier's work to do. They are here to give you strength and discipline and steel; to impress on you the importance of strategy and planning, which you are going to need in days to come."

Which mystified me even more, as I had always considered myself the most unlikely soldier imaginable.

My final act as a National Serviceman, the day after meeting Lord Alexander, was to attend an *al fresco* regimental tea party during which, before eating, I drank rather too many large gins and tonic, sat at the feet of the Colonel's wife, paid her elaborate compliments, strolled over to the bandmaster, congratulated him on his choice of music, headed for the nearest rhododendron bush and collapsed into it – out cold. Apparently, four of my fellow subalterns carried me back to our quarters, which were under canvas.

Next morning the Adjutant severely reprimanded me, but the Colonel, bless him, suppressing a smile, saved the day by volunteering that his wife had seemed to be flattered and rather amused by my reckless attentions.

iv

The power behind the Throne

Throughout history, kings, emperors, pharaohs and heads of State have used secret advisers. The Egyptian pharaohs are known to have employed astrologers; the Caesars, soothsayers; Queen Elizabeth I was advised by the mysterious Dr John Dee, whose code-name, believe it or not, was 007. Other celebrated seers were Merlin, Cagliostro, the far-sighted Michel de Notre Dame (Nostradamus), the Count of Saint Germain and, during the last century, the 'sleeping prophet', Edgar Cayce.

It is common knowledge that Hitler was instructed – some might say controlled – by a sinister group whose dream was the emergence, at whatever cost, of an Aryan super-race.

Winston Churchill also had an occult adviser throughout World War II, who urged him to introduce 'the Silent Minute': at 9 o'clock each evening, people throughout Britain sat by their radios, quietly thinking of peace and victory before the evening news was broadcast. Hitler, who knew a thing or two about the power of collective thought and invocation, was furious: he called it, "Britain's secret weapon".

Julius Caesar ignored the soothsayer who warned him to beware the Ides of March. John Kennedy is said to have disregarded repeated warnings from the celebrated seer Jeanne Dixon regarding his fateful trip to Dallas, Texas. Both men paid the ultimate price.

Today, Intelligence agencies and police use mediums and psychics to locate missing persons, intercept consignments of drugs and monitor illicit activities.

I myself had dramatic proof of this in January, 1969.

Two friends of mine, Lillian and Maureen, both highly-gifted psychics, who did not know each other, telephoned me during the same week to report that they had 'seen' Prince Charles lying at the feet of the Queen at some formal State function.

One of them had seen him surrounded by "a ring of fire"; the other told me she had seen castle battlements and a man with a machine-gun.

As both women had an excellent record of accurate precognition, I wrote to the Duke of Edinburgh to report what they had seen. I suggested that security round Prince Charles should be intensified, especially during the Investiture that was to take place at Caernarvon Castle in six months' time, during which he would become the Prince of Wales.

The Duke acknowledged my letter and, a day or so later, the press announced that the guard on Prince Charles, who was still an undergraduate at Trinity College, Cambridge, had been doubled.

Seven weeks later, Special Branch captured several members of a Welsh extremist group whose banners read, **'Free Wales from English domination'**, and who were preparing to make their moves at the forthcoming Investiture.

I can only presume they intended to put on English army uniforms, and one or two of them would somehow have made their way up onto the roof of the Castle. Among the arms and ammunition captured were Lugers and Mausers (German hand-guns), grenades – *and a machine-gun.*

Although history records that the Scottish, Irish and Welsh peoples have all been treated outrageously by English governments in the past, and all three nations are fully justified in their desire for independence, I remain unconvinced that murder is the means to achieve political or social ends.

In any case, it is an unwritten rule that if you are given information from inner sources regarding someone's health, well-being, safety or survival, it is your duty to pass on that information – if not to the person concerned, to someone who might be in a position to transmute or avert what has been foreseen.

Nearly thirty years later, as I took my seat behind her family in the north transept of Westminster Abbey, on the morning of Diana's funeral, something rather astonishing occurred to me.

If those two women had *not* had their visions – and had the Intelligence services not been prompted by these and, presumably, other warnings to conduct an intensive search for sources of possible danger – there might never have been a Charles, Prince of Wales.

And if *he* had been cut down on that day, there would never have been a Diana, Princess of Wales, either.

V

We're off to see the Wizard

O N MIDSUMMER DAY, 1974, some friends and I visited Park
Wood in Somerset, at the centre of what is called 'the
Glastonbury Zodiac'.

Deep in the heart of the wood we decided to split up, and agreed
to meet in half an hour, to exchange reports.

I found myself in a little sunlit glade – slender birches in an
approximate circle, knee-high grass, tall clusters of wildflowers;
midges dancing through the still air. The silence was absolute.

I closed my eyes and tried to still my mind.

Why were we here – trespassing, probably – in the heart of a
small, private wood?

Because one of the first recorded references to this Zodiac – in
which the symbols of all twelve constellations have been 'drawn'
on the land, using roads, hedges and other natural features – was
made by Dr John Dee, magician and adviser to Queen Elizabeth I.
He called it 'Merlin's Secret'.

And a week or so before our expedition, while reading Anthony
Roberts' *Atlantean Traditions in Ancient Britain*, I came across these
words:

> "... *the exact centre point of this Zodiac is found at tiny Park
> Wood on the outskirts of the village of Butleigh. It is here that
> seekers may one day unearth a miracle. The long slumber of
> Blake's 'Giant Albion' is now drawing to a close, and the
> revelation of new life is rising like the first stirrings of a late
> spring* ..."

I can't explain it, but those words seemed to be an invitation. A summons, almost. Right then and there, I knew something was going to come of it.

Without warning, a voice broke the silence in the little glade where I now stood, deep in thought:

> *"Do not seek Excalibur on the physical plane, my friend. The places where we worked still carry our vibrations, but over the centuries the true power has been stored and guarded on the inner planes.*
>
> *"Only when groups lie yours are attuned to the highest pitch will you be able to unlock some of the power that is still available — for correct use."*

I stood rooted to the spot, my heart pounding. A flush of excitement rose to my cheeks. The voice was as clear as if someone had spoken beside me.

But it had come from inside my own head.

It was the Magician himself, of that I am convinced. Some things just *are*, and that voice had been Merlin's.

I hurried back to my companions, blithely unaware of the train of events that had just been set in motion, and where it was going to lead in time to come.

In the years that followed, Merlin was to become an indispensable guide, tutor and friend. There was nothing remote or impersonal about him or his communications – which we soon came to recognise by their unique blend of compassion and dispassion, utter candour and uproarious good humour.

For all that, he was extremely outspoken on the subject of man's outrageous attitude to women and his treatment of them; and equally scathing about our callous abuse of "your mother, Earth, who, uncomplaining, supplies your every need."

He several times urged us to treat him as an equal, as we would an elder brother, and not to hold him in awe.

"You do not always have to agree with me," he would say. "Truth is a many-splendoured thing; have opinions of your own."

In June 1977 he said to me, "I shall prepare an objective vision for your eyes alone. Be prepared . . ."

A week or two later, my chums and I visited Chalice Well garden, at the foot of Glastonbury Tor. It was hot, so we sprawled on the small lawn for a while in silence.

I was lying on my back, shielding my eyes from the sun, when a small mottled bird flew into my field of vision and began to hover directly above me at about forty feet.

A Merlin hawk.

The first shock hit my solar plexus.

It was the exact shape of a Spitfire!

Then a second shock.

I remembered that the Spitfire was powered by the Rolls Royce 'Merlin' engine! And played a vital role in saving Britain in 1940. For a moment I lay there, transfixed, unable to speak or move.

The hawk, having delivered its message, dipped its wings and flew off over Chalice Hill.

As soon as I could, I visited my friend Peter Quiller, who had become our 'channel' to the Magician, and asked Merlin if he had inspired Mitchell to design the Spitfire during Britain's 'darkest hour', and also Sir Henry Royce and his engineers, who built the Merlin engine.

He chuckled and, in his deep unmistakable voice, which sounds like nothing so much as thunder rolling down the lower slopes of a mountain, replied, *"Why do you ask questions whose answers you already know?!"*

It was the most benevolent reprimand you could ever wish to hear.

vi
A message from the Magician

ONE SUMMER EVENING IN 1992, I was thinking about the extraordinary cards that life had dealt the star-crossed Diana and Prince Charles — fame, wealth, power and privilege on the one hand; sorrow, loneliness, vulnerability and extreme frustration on the other — when I felt the unmistakable presence of Merlin at my shoulder.

He wished me to send a personal message to Diana, he said, and another, separately, to Prince Charles. I did as asked. And this is what the Magician had to say to Diana:

For the Princess of Wales:

Yours is a difficult path, dear lady, a lonely path. For those who lead, the way is never easy. Yet remember, *you* chose this journey, long before you were born.

Even then, you knew the rewards would be more than matched by obstacles, setbacks and disappointments.

You are undergoing the ordeal that those with a great purpose must endure — such is the requirement of the inner law.

In recent years, with increasing frequency and intensity, you have been asking yourself, "What must I do? How can I best serve the people of these islands — and the wider world beyond?"

The answer lies where it has always lain —
within yourself.

The light and power that radiate from
the Crown are perceived by most people
as something awesome and remote. But
you have already revealed that the Crown
reflects the *inner* light, the *inner* power
that is the birthright not of a privileged
few, but of all mankind.

With an instinct that is truly royal, you
have used your hard-won strength to uplift
and encourage those less fortunate than
yourself.

That chapter is almost over, and another is
about to begin. As you are doubtless aware,
this is not just the end of one century and the
beginning of another — it is the end of one
world and the beginning of another. And you
yourself — should you so desire — shall play a
crucial role in this transition . . .

You are *not* alone. Beside your countless
friends and admirers on Earth (no-one has
ever possessed as vast a private army as your
own!) a great company of souls is watching
over you in the heaven worlds, sustaining
you, holding you in the Light.

Your trials and initiations have been many
and cruel — but you will rise above them in
triumph.

What you achieve will eclipse all the long,
dark hours of solitude, self-doubt and despair —
and you will finally know that all the pain
and sacrifice have been worthwhile.

"M"

vii

The Dragon King

I started in the morning, went through the day,
then had dinner, and then I went back there and worked
till — I don't know — one or two o'clock in the morning.
It sort of unveiled itself. I was the stenographer.
I could hear them. I could hear them, literally.

Arthur Miller
Describing the process of writing
the first act of Death Of A Salesman

JUST BEFORE CHRISTMAS in 1992, I was talking on the phone to Ellen Easton — a worldly-wise Scotswoman who for some years had provided me with an invaluable 'outside line' to inner worlds — when out of the blue, in mid-sentence, she said:

"Hold it a moment. Merlin's telling me he's got a gift for you. A ring. A regent ring."

"Great," I said. "Would you thank him, and tell him I look forward to receiving it."

Weeks went by, then months, and still no ring — which was highly unusual because, believe me, Merlin never makes promises he doesn't keep.

Then one day next spring, a good friend, Molly Daubeny, invited me to the preview of Richard Eyre's memorable, sinister production of *Macbeth* at the National Theatre in London.

We took our seats in the Olivier Theatre, the house lights went down and on came the three weird sisters to do their thing with the cauldron. Without warning, a ring of fire, some fifteen feet in diameter, leapt out of the ground and surrounded them.

And in that nanosecond, knowing we were in for three hours or so of unrelieved murder, mayhem and intrigue, I knew I *had* to write the complete opposite – a novel about the spirit and essence of Britain, about the ancient magic and lore for which these islands were once famed, but which slowly faded from sight and memory when the nation turned to outward adventure, exploration and 'the Great Game' of Empire.

But that's not all. In that same split-second, *the whole story* came into my mind – the way compressed data is sent by Modem down a phone line to a computer, which receives and stores it for subsequent decoding.

That night I got home, switched on my word-processor and went to work. For the next five, feverish days and nights – a burst of almost white-hot exertion in which I found myself surrounded by what I can only describe as a column of pale fire, intense but without heat or ferocity – I worked flat out to nail the thing down.

As you may know, most writing is as laborious as mining – you sweat away in the dark, hour after hour, hacking great lumps out of the rock-face or clay, then haul up bucketsful of the stuff, hoping you're going to find the occasional nugget or gem lurking in it somewhere. But occasionally, as you might have heard – or experienced for yourself – inspiration comes in a rush; and, when it does, you just have to sit tight and hold on to your hat until the hurricane blows over.

But I digress. In the screenplay, Merlin takes us back to the 6th century and shows us what happened behind the scenes, setting in motion the events that have since entered into legend and folklore.

We learn why the Magician would not allow Arthur to be brought up in the palace of his father, Uther Pendragon, High King of Greater Britain. We watch Merlin secretly training Arthur for kingship, then see him champion the young Prince – in the teeth of opposition from the Court, and from other contenders – when Uther dies, leaving the Throne empty.

And the title of the piece is . . .

The Dragon King, subtitled *The Ring of Fire*.

So my regent ring *had* arrived, after all! Thanks, Merlin.

viii
The Princess

THE MOMENT THE SCRIPT was finished, it occurred to me that of all people, the Princess of Wales – who had graciously accepted my last two books – should see *The Dragon King*. She, after all, was the mother – and, therefore, largely responsible for the emotional and spiritual education – of a young man who will probably be King of England one day; and she too, to say the least, had her problems and her enemies, the Palace having closed ranks on her after her separation and divorce from the Prince of Wales. She was now virtually living in exile in her own country, having to depend on the considerable reserves of goodwill acquired during her glory years.

She was kind enough to accept the screenplay – which encouraged me to say I hoped she would read it to her sons, William and Harry, one day – and less than a week later, by the most extraordinary coincidence, the entire front page of *The Mail On Sunday* was given over to a news story headlined:

CONCERN FOR THE PRINCES
Member of Parliament urges the Prime Minister to ensure that the Princes' futures should be monitored by a group of wise men, independent experts who are as powerful as the Palace.

Some coincidence! Evidently the issues dealt with in *The Dragon King* are as alive today as they were 1400 years ago. And although we've undoubtedly come a long, long way, scientifically and technologically, since those far-off days, in many other respects we don't seem to have advanced at all.

Whichever way you look at it, the desperate struggle Merlin and

Arthur had, to inject a little chivalry, gallantry and fair play into the public consciousness, slap-bang in the middle of the Dark Ages, bears an uncomfortable resemblance to the problems the Western world is facing today.

After a grim decade of smash-and-grab, snout-in-the-trough economics – the soulless, heartless 1980s, presided over by those two tin gods, monetarism and market forces – what are our kids going to turn into, if *we* no longer believe in anything?

And as for the business of attempting to weld the British Isles into a *united* kingdom – or mankind into one family, for that matter – it remains as daunting a problem today as it was to Merlin, Arthur and the Companions of the Round Table then.

A little later, I wrote to encourage the increasingly isolated Princess as she pursued her quest:

> "What everyone seems to have forgotten is that, long before the days of warrior Kings and royal dynasties serving political and territorial ends, the purpose of Kings and Queens was to embody certain universal principles:

the King:	order, justice, courage, fatherhood, leadership
the Queen:	love, wisdom, beauty, intuition, motherhood, mercy (mercy being an attribute the King would probably learn from his Queen)
the Magician:	creative intelligence, strategy, far-sightedness (Kings and Queens always had their Magician or counsellor, whom they consulted when the occasion arose)

"Not forgetting the fourth member of this group: the Mystic, or Master of Ceremonies as I prefer to call him, who was responsible for ceremonial and music and dance. He is sometimes identified as the joker or clown, the lord of misrule – employed by the Court to lighten the mood in cold or stuffy palaces!"

Despite the many obstacles that beset her, and her own private misgivings, in her public life Diana became the living embodiment of the queenly virtues listed above. Which is doubtless why she became – and still is – the Queen of Hearts to so many people around the world.

And as for the Master of Ceremonies, there was never any shortage of music and dance and fun and laughter in her life, to offset the burden of her pain and loneliness.

ix

"Enjoy the roller-coaster ride . . ."

23 January 1996
Private & confidential
HRH The Princess of Wales
St James's Palace
SW1

Dear Diana,

A while ago you were kind enough to accept a copy of a screenplay I had just written – *The Dragon King* – in which Merlin is seen training the young Prince Arthur for kingship, and later fights for Arthur's right to succeed his father to the Throne. I hope you enjoyed it, and that one day your sons will also get some enjoyment, inspiration and amusement from it. One day, I hope it will be made into a film . . .

And now to the purpose of this letter. You probably have a larger 'family' of friends and admirers than any other person in Britain – or anywhere else, for that matter. And this huge family recognise and appreciate your gifts, your work and your courage.

What your detractors appear to have forgotten is that, long ago, the Pharaoh, Emperor or monarch was, in every sense, a priest/king, leading by example. The spiritual aspect of his reign was paramount; more worldly, material considerations were secondary.

The Pharaoh Akhenaten was a notable example, and Alexander the Great another; King Arthur a third – and although Arthur was betrayed and his mission was sabotaged, the events of his life survive to this very day in our collective memory, and in our yearning for a better world.

So it must have really infuriated your critics when the duckling grew into a fully-fledged swan and, with the natural skills and graces that owe nothing to the instruction of chamberlains and courtiers, put them all to shame by demonstrating the *true* virtues of royalty – and in so doing, won for herself an unassailable place in people's hearts.

Although they have caused you a lot of grief and pain, I'm sure you'll find it in your heart to forgive them, critics and enemies alike, and to let them go. 'Cutting the ties that bind', as you know, is a loving and forgiving act that frees *both* parties to continue their lives with much of the tension and conflict resolved, most of the pain transmuted.

Everything that is happening, however painful, has a hidden purpose, and this will empower you to discard the heavy emotional luggage that has accumulated around you in recent years. Now is the moment to go into training for the *next* chapter, light of heart and light of step.

I'm sure it gives you great comfort to know that *everyone* who is aware of the significance of this moment in human affairs, and who is preparing to play his or her role in days to come is, like yourself, in the 'furnace' right now, all dross being burned off.

No doubt about it – our steel is being tested in the fires, and this isn't a comfortable process – in fact it's darn painful! But hang in there a little longer, and soon you'll be walking taller than ever. Everyone will notice a subtle but powerful change: a greater serenity, increased inner strength and poise.

Meanwhile, enjoy the roller-coaster ride! This is, in many ways, the most crucial moment in human history. "The Grand Audit" is Merlin's way of describing it, by which he means the wholesale clearing up of all our debts – at every level, from the personal to the national – and the balancing of the books before the next phase begins.

And what a vital role young people are about to play in this drama! "These children who are *not* children have come to take their planet back," Merlin once said to us, back in the mid-1970s — words we've never been able to forget. And if we can't show *them* the way — who knows, maybe our children will show *us*!

For several years now, we've been researching and developing a kids' project — *Our World Summit* — in which young people of various nationalities will take their places at a Round Table (!), take an Oath of Allegiance and promise to tackle some of the biggest problems confronting us all. They'll invite kids everywhere to enlist in what we hope and believe will grow into the biggest civil taskforce ever known . . .

Time will tell!

The Grail?

This time round, we've been encouraged to look for a *new* Grail, a world Grail. In other words, a symbol or ideal that transcends language, politics, philosophy, culture, tradition — even the great religions themselves — and embraces us *all*.

Please accept my warmest good wishes at this cold, grey and dispiriting time of year. If only some bright spark could come up with a way of towing the British Isles to the Mediterranean, or maybe somewhere off the coast of South Africa!

Love from
Michael

X

Awesome Welles (ii)

I'm going to build me a stairway to Paradise,
with a new step every day . . .

George Gershwin

IN THE AUTUMN OF 1996, in the Samuel French bookshop on Sunset Boulevard, I caught sight of a biography of Orson Welles, opened it and looked for a reference to *The Bible*. It was there. I turned to the relevant page – and got quite a shock.

Orson had chosen the story of Jacob, in Genesis, and had written his own script. So I would have been playing the leading character as a young man!

When I got back to our office – which was directly opposite Orson's former house at the foot of the Hollywood Hills! – I found a Bible, looked up the story of Jacob, which I confess I had never read before, and after a few verses, there it was:

10 Jacob left Beer-sheba, and went towards Haran.

11 And he came to a certain place, and stayed there that night, because the sun had set. Taking one of the stones of the place, he put it under his head and lay down in that place to sleep.

12 *And he dreamed that there was a ladder set up on the earth, and the top of it reached to heaven;*

13 *and behold, the angels of God were ascending and descending on it . . .*

(my italics)

"In the week between her death and her funeral,
she won the greatest victory any human being
has ever won on Earth – a strategic victory,
a moral victory and a spiritual victory.
The rage of her enemies and
the celebration of
those who
loved her – and still love
her – was only to be expected."

Richard Heritage
August, 2002

PART 1

A Matter of Life and 'Death'

Death doesn't frighten me

Diana, to a friend

I died as a mineral and became a plant.
I died as a plant and rose to animal.
I died as animal and became human.
Why should I fear?
When was I less by dying?
Yet once more I shall die human,
To soar with angels blessed above.
And when I sacrifice my angel soul
I shall become what no mind ever conceived.

From the Persian poet **Rumi Jalaluddin,**
a Sufi Muslim, frequently said as a prayer at bedtime.

A glimpse of Paradise

Honey, I'm home! My God, what a blast!
No rent, no bills, no pain, no-one hassling me.
I go where I want and see who I want and do what I want.
And I'm getting younger every day!
How about them apples?!

Ava Gardner
1991

I CLOSED MY EYES and there was Diana, in a honey-coloured suit with a short, tight skirt, sun-tanned bare legs, her hair gilded by what appeared to be late afternoon sunlight. At least, that's what I saw – but I got the distinct impression that I was seeing what she felt I'd be comfortable with; that she was veiled in some way, and I wasn't seeing her in her entirety, her fully ascended state. The landscape behind her was shimmering copper and gold. I hesitated, but she held out her hand, so I stepped out of Regent's Park and into heaven. It was as easy as that . . .

She noticed the expression of wonder on my face, and my blissed-out state. All I could say was, "Wow."

She grinned. "It's the same for everyone – and these are only the lowlands, by the way. When you get here, a wave of happiness and relief all rolled into one hits you like an express train, and you want to shout and scream and laugh and whirl round and dance like a mad thing – which is exactly what I did when I first got here!"

I nodded. I felt very much the same myself. And I couldn't help noticing that although she was speaking to me, her lips weren't moving – it must be her thoughts I was hearing; she wasn't speaking out loud.

"Let's walk for a bit, and I'll tell you something about what I've discovered since I got back."

She indicated our surroundings.

"Just like the physical Universe, this dimension – which some people call 'Paradise', and you can see why, can't you? – is simply an idea of God's which He / She has thought about so intensely that it's taken form and substance and colour – and now has an independent existence of its own. Just like all the other levels, or heavens."

She slid her hand into mine, and I have to tell you the tears were pouring down my face, because she and the place were both so extraordinarily beautiful.

"Even this place can't hold a candle to the highlands of heaven," she continued. "Just *thinking* about them is enough to knock you out – literally; the vibrations up there are so high that no-one in human form can take them."

She looked around us again. "But who'd want any more than all this? A place where everything is perfect, and seems to have been created specifically to delight, fulfil and satisfy *you*. The gardens and parks, the skies, the colours and scents are what you'd choose for yourself – *if* you had the talent and the imagination to dream them up!"

I nodded. Take the most beautiful landscape on Earth you can possibly imagine, and multiply it by a factor of ten – and you'll have just a faint idea why they call this place Paradise . . .

The scene faded.

I opened my eyes, and was back in Regent's Park. The setting sun glinted through the avenue of trees beside the fountain. It was getting cold. I got to my feet and headed for the Inner Circle and the lake, where geese and swans scrounge for bread from passers-by.

And believe me, several minutes elapsed before the power and the glory of the other place began to fade . . .

To the reader

I'VE BEEN DYING to have a word with you ever since my 'death', so-called. But now that we've cleared *that* one up – that there isn't any death, as a lot of you already knew or suspected; and if I *were* dead, I wouldn't be writing this book, would I?! – you have no idea how good it is to be able to talk to you, and to share some of my thoughts with you.

If you're reading this, I assume it's either because you're one of my friends or acquaintances, or a member of the huge 'family' I didn't know personally, who were good enough to wish me well when I was living 'down there' – as we call it 'up here' – and who still think kindly of me.

I hope you won't mind if I don't talk about lunches at *San Lorenzo*, good hair days, bad hair days, bulimia, anorexia, work-outs in the gym, my search for love, my mistakes – yes, there *were* rather a lot of them, as my critics have so often pointed out! – or my relationship with the press and the Royal family. That's all been done to death.

No, this is a very special privilege I have been given – can you *imagine* how many people up here want to do what I'm doing right now? – and I don't want to waste it.

One of the first things that happened when we were back on our feet – it took quite a while before we had fully recovered from the shock and violence of our sudden 'exit' – was that they showed me the thousands of cards and letters people had written, *and* some of the thoughts they were thinking at the time.

I was invited to a kind of private viewing theatre, and your thoughts appeared on a screen in neat columns, with various subjects and emotions in different colours. Who had gone to all the trouble of arranging them like that, I haven't the faintest idea – but they had.

I was absolutely amazed how many of you were asking if my work was finished – and if not, would I please return to finish it!

I have visited my sons and family and loved ones, of course, and tried to get them to hear and feel my thoughts and wishes and hopes and apologies and, above all, my love. Sometimes they knew I was there, and quite often they didn't.

I often 'tune in', to keep up with what's happening on Earth. I have re-visited all the places I loved most in England and around the world, *and* many of the places where there's still such pain and tragedy. They are the most unforgettable of all. That's why it's so exciting that so many people in every country have put aside part of their time and energy, and are doing everything they can to 'turn things round' for the better.

We're not allowed to interfere with you and what you're doing – it's against the Law. But nothing can stop us sending you our thoughts and good wishes, and trying to pass on useful information and ideas to anyone whose 'receiver' is switched on. So we do!

This book is part of that work. And whether I knew you or not, it comes with my love and thanks and best wishes. And not only mine, but everyone else's 'up here' too.

Please don't think 'up here' means we think we're superior, and 'down there' means 'inferior' – I'm talking wavelengths, dimensions, not making comparisons. And remember, we might seem to be a long way away, but that's just an illusion. In fact we're only a thought away.

Which reminds me: not long ago, I heard someone on the radio say, "It's time we let Diana rest in peace."

Peace?!

Believe me, I have never been busier!

7

All that 'Rest In Peace' nonsense was a deliberate – and highly successful – attempt by the Church to keep the doors to heaven locked and bolted; to persuade us all that there's no life after 'death', so-called – or if there is, it's a no-go area strictly reserved for saints, angels and the Almighty himself. And that only on 'Judgement Day' will the graves give up their dead . . .

What a pack of lies! They should be ashamed of themselves. Maybe, secretly, they are. Never mind – truth, like water, has a way of finding its way through even the tiniest cracks, and in recent years, millions of cracks have appeared in the gates of heaven, and the Light shining through them is getting stronger every day.

Thank God for that. And thank all the people who have spent their lives – have even given their lives – trying to undo all the damage.

Every year the spiritual kingdom
and the human kingdom draw ever closer together,
in preparation for the great coming fusion.

Vera Stanley Alder
The Initiation of the World
1939

1

First things first

It is critical that we find a way to bring about rapid,
sweeping change of human consciousness and actions
worldwide — something that enables us to provoke a large-
scale shift of course in a very short time.

Mikhail Gorbachev

THE VERY FIRST THING I'd like to say is that the *real* history of
the human race is totally unlike anything we've ever been
told. I know this is going to upset a lot of people, but the fact is
that we have all been deliberately misled, and have come to
believe the lies we've been told. And who can blame us? No-one
has ever told us the truth! It's certainly going to infuriate those
who did the lying in the first place, wherever they are now, *and*
the people who are still protecting those lies today, because they
know no better.

And as for those who *know* they've been selling us shoddy goods
all along — well I wouldn't like to be in *their* shoes when the
reckoning comes!

As some of you know, there are planetary databanks up here.
Everything that has ever happened on Earth is recorded in
hologram form. I have been shown glimpses of our real history,
and believe me, it's much closer to *Star Wars* than the fairy stories
in the Old Testament. The 'God' who created Adam and Eve

wasn't the Almighty, he was a renegade, carrying out one of many colonisations that have occurred on this planet.

I'm sure most of us have asked ourselves at one time or another, "Why are the nations always at war? Why is it virtually impossible to introduce peace on Earth? Why are we always spying on each other, building huge stockpiles of weapons, preparing for the worst?"

There are many answers to those questions, and here are just a few that I have come across recently:

First, because the 'god' who created this experiment *wants* us to be constantly at war with each other ('Divide and conquer' seems to be his motto); second, because war enables nations to expand and create empires, virtually unchallenged; and third, because war is big business. Right now, it's one of the top three in the world.

The fourth reason is a real humdinger, and it's simply this: because war is men's business, and women have always let men persuade them that it makes sense to leave the running of war and 'defence' and economics and industry and government to *them* (the men).

Result? Several thousand years of highly profitable wars and Empires, organised by men — whose women and children have had to watch from the sidelines, wondering when and if the madness and bloodshed will ever stop.

I have been asked not to be too outspoken, to be as diplomatic as I can, but I'm sorry — enough is enough. It's time for a little plain speaking here, and if that means stepping on a few people's toes, then so be it. I can hear them now:

"Who *is* this ignorant young woman? What does *she* know about our business?"

"Business" is right — that's *exactly* what it is. The dirtiest business ever devised by man: human butchery. Maybe now you can appreciate that the 'women's movement' isn't just about equal pay and equal opportunities, and never was. It's about ending these needless massacres once and for all, and introducing another kind of life altogether on Earth.

Open your eyes! All around you are hundreds of millions of people who have had pain, fear, drudgery and sacrifice up to here. They want *another* kind of life – and they're going to have it.

Nothing and no-one can stop them. Why? Because enough people on Earth are now consciously calling for change to make that change possible.

I'm not talking instant change, of course; nor am I talking about some pop-up Utopia where birds sing and the sun shines all day long. But I *am* talking about a world where no-one goes without, and there's justice, freedom, equality and peace of mind.

They say that in a world of duality there has to be light and dark. Well, yes – but I have never bought the idea that there's *got* to be poverty, *got* to be cruelty, *got* to be victims. There's enough opportunity and food and shelter for *everyone on Earth*. And if they tell you there isn't, they're lying.

Earth was *not* designed to be a detention centre, but that's what it has become – thanks to some extremely high-handed decisions made long ago by a number of so-called exalted beings who should have – and almost certainly did – know better. People are being deprived of their civil liberties every day – even in the so-called 'democracies' of the world.

The desire to control others, to keep them under surveillance, is a sickness, a disease of the mind. May I respectfully remind the President of the United States and Britain's Prime Minister that 'democracy' means 'rule by the people' – *not* control of the people by governments. And 'Republic' means 'the thing of the people; the matter, the concern, the business of the public.' (Okay, so I've been doing my homework – better late than never!)

Sorry, gentlemen, but the prime directive here (at planetary HQ, since you ask) is to wake mankind from its drugged sleep; to remind you all of your rights as galactic beings and as co-creators of Creation. *No-one* should have to live in distress, poverty, disease or fear. And the good news is that they won't have to, for much longer.

But that was then, and this is now. And now for a little good news: everywhere there are signs that the nightmare is soon to end. We'll speak again soon, and I'll tell you what I mean.

2

Turnaround

Mankind is in a desperate situation.
How can we break out of it?

Akira Kurosawa
Film director
Arena, BBC2

D URING THE LAST CENTURY, literally hundreds of thousands of petitions were sent up to Supreme HQ (I can't think of any other way of describing God's domain) from every country on Earth, asking for some kind of reprieve or Divine intervention. So I know you'll be delighted to hear that, because things have got so out of balance, and so many lives are now at risk, *and* so many systems are reaching breaking-point – don't look now, but civilisation itself is facing meltdown – permission has at last been granted for a number of adjustments or refinements to be made to the original Plan.

You're probably wondering why some kind of emergency measures weren't introduced much sooner, once things had begun to go seriously wrong. I have often wondered as much myself.

Well, it wasn't a cold, callous and heartless decision – it was considered that, as all these crises and emergencies provided mankind with a number of serious challenges, they might just speed up the process of spiritualising the planet – which happens to be the primary task of the human race, by the way – so things could be left as they are.

A lot of people will argue that *no* plan that calls for such wholesale human sacrifice is tolerable – and I have to say I'm with you all the way. But as there's no such thing as death, ultimately we're talking about enforced separation here, not extermination.

But even *that* doesn't excuse the callous way 'ordinary' human beings have been used by the warlords and conquerors down the ages! Or how cheap physical life has become on Earth.

I have been shown a kind of video of the world in years to come – a projection based on all available data plus all known probabilities – and I am allowed to tell you that huge change is coming; almost all of it very positive indeed. Some of the changes will be unsettling, unnerving even, but once everyone has got used to them, things will quickly settle down. It begins in fits and starts almost immediately, and gathers momentum in the second decade of this century. The year 2012 should see several major leaps forward.

How do you turn a heavily-armed camp with all kinds of perimeter defences and booby-traps into a playground for people of all ages?

Good question. It certainly isn't going to be easy. *Unless* it suddenly occurs to all the men guarding the camp that there's nothing to fear inside the enclosure *or* beyond the perimeter – and that all the weaponry and sophisticated security systems are a waste of time, energy and money.

That realisation is about to dawn on all those men* and their superiors at approximately the same time, so there'll be no need for any more nightmare scenarios of armed forces at loggerheads with their superior officers.

Maybe you're already thinking "are you seriously trying to tell me that all the men and women who make up the military, naval and air Establishments of the world – who obviously believe that what they're doing is essential if their countries are to remain safe

---

* (Okay, there *are* a number of women involved as well, but men are very much in the majority here.)

and protected – are going to have this simultaneous revelation that what they're doing is no longer necessary?

"And are you saying that all the power-brokers and wheeler-dealers of the world are suddenly going to *stop* power-broking and wheeling and dealing?! Sorry, but it just doesn't add up at all, whichever way you look at it."

No, it doesn't. *If* the world is to remain as it is.

But it isn't.

The nightmare is almost over. And that's a promise.

It's about be demonstrated – to most people's satisfaction, anyway (you can't please everyone) – that there *is* no death. Which makes two things much clearer:

i.   We all 'do time' on Earth, then return home;
ii. Earth is a kind of floating university, where we can gain experience and strength of character by having to deal with the kind of obstacles and problems that are unique to the physical world.

As the truth about the 'higher' worlds gradually faded from human memory – I am told that long ago it was common knowledge – and we began to believe that life on Earth was all there is, we started to act out of fear, to use force if intimidation didn't do the trick, to stake our claim to more and more territory, to grab whatever the Earth had to offer, whether we needed it or not; and, last but not least, to dream up more and more ways of controlling other people.

And so it has gone on and on, until no-one is safe any more. We all lock our homes; we're all frightened of being attacked in the street; we're all scrabbling around trying to make money, to hoard more food and possessions than we'll ever need, to outsmart the next guy; to insulate ourselves physically, emotionally and in every other way from the outside world with all its craziness, insecurity and danger.

How revealing that the symbol of America itself used to be the phoenix — a creature that emerged from the fire unharmed, and soared away into the sky — until someone decided to replace it with the more predatory eagle!

But now the truth is dawning.

We have nothing, and no-one, to be afraid of! We're no longer cavemen, fighting off gigantic lizards, we're sophisticated people who can photograph bacteria and send probes to the stars. We're all aboard a single spacecraft, so we're literally 'all in this thing together'. And if we are all pulling *for* each other, rather than competing against each other, suddenly we're surrounded by six or seven billion *allies* instead of six or seven billion enemies or rivals!

In other words, remove the danger, remove the fear — and the need for all this self-protection vanishes. And I am here to tell you that there really will be no more reason to be frightened, once we have turnaround — which is only moments away now, on the hands of the cosmic clock.

The sleeping giant is about to wake — and that giant is mankind itself . . .

3

Things to come

*Take heart: you are not outcasts on
a small planet, drifting aimlessly in Space.
The Earth is only one starship in an immense fleet
that is turning the corner and
sailing back to Glory.*

Merlin

A S I JUST SAID, I have been given a privileged peek behind the curtain, and been shown some of the amazing things that are about to change human life out of all recognition.

They were all made possible because scientists up here have always realised that *everything* is energy of one kind or another, and that even the densest 'matter', ourselves included, isn't solid at all, so they haven't been sidetracked into dreaming up mechanical devices when other, more sophisticated solutions are available.

My whirlwind tour of the new territory – through laboratories and workshops that are filled with light and music and laughter, rather than heavy machinery – literally left my head spinning, so I asked my new friend, who took me on the tour, to explain some of the things I had just been shown, in a language that people like me, who aren't scientifically-minded, can understand.

Here is just a quick taste, or appetiser, taken from the catalogue of goodies that are being prepared for the human race:

Contact between 'heaven', so-called, and Earth will eventually be as simple and natural as calling a friend long-distance on a telephone . . .

The money system is going to change out of all recognition — *no-one need ever be poor again!* Housing and clothing and education will be free. Food too, believe it or not . . .

Education is going to go through such a transformation that you'll be wondering why the new system wasn't introduced centuries ago. Classes will be as enjoyable as anything kids do in their leisure time . . .

And as for science and technology! The things I've been shown verge on the miraculous. There'll be no need to drive around in clunky metal boxes driven by oil and petrol; no more traffic jams; no more hunger or disease; no more surveillance, eavesdropping and mind control . . .

Gravity will be harnessed. Just think what *that's* going to do to all forms of transport. Crime? Crime is the way that people get their revenge on a society that promises them little or nothing. And who can blame them? A society gets the criminals it deserves. The crueller it is, the more desperate its criminals are going to be. But soon, *all the injustices will have gone* — and crime along with them . . .

Impossible? Just you wait and see!

4

The coat of many colours

ONE OF THE FIRST THINGS I began to understand, when I'd settled in and got my strength back and reviewed my recent life, was that we are all *many* people at the same time.

There's our personality, the person people around us see and hear and get to know – the tip of the iceberg, so to speak; then there's our emotional self, part hidden, part on show; our thought self – a private person living in a private world that is mostly off limits even to those around us; our intelligence, which reveals *how* we think and how we deal with life and all its challenges and opportunities; then there's our character – the sum of our virtues and faults, the 'real' us, which shows itself in the way we handle our relationships and crises and pressures; and above and beyond all of these different aspects or personalities, we have our soul or spirit.

And then of course there's fame. To protect themselves, or to help them do a good professional job, famous people often develop a public persona which has very little in common with their private self.

Marilyn Monroe is the classic example. Just like all the roles she played in her films, 'Marilyn' was a fictional character too, invented by Norma Jean and her studio – a peroxide blonde sex goddess, a living doll, childlike, available, photogenic and oh so easy to merchandise.

19

But who went home at night? Who had the love affairs, the anxieties, the relationships and the studios and producers to deal with? Yes, Norma Jean.

And poor Rita Hayworth. "They all wanted to sleep with Gilda," she said, "and they were so disappointed when all they got was me." Even the gorgeous Rita couldn't compete with herself in her most famous film role — as *Gilda*.

When I appeared in public, I tried my level best to *be* a Princess, to be what everyone expected me to be. And whatever I gave people when visiting hospitals and war zones was more than repaid by the love and affection I got from *them*: it was very much two-way traffic. But when I got home and took off the power clothes and jewels and put on a tracksuit and trainers, I was just Diana, a young woman with all the doubts and insecurities that every other young woman has — and several more besides. On really bad days I felt empty, alone, almost lost. Sometimes I even feared for my sanity.

My actor friends used to tell me not to worry, it's always like that — the final curtain and the explosion of applause, the glitter and glamour of film premieres, instant recognition in the streets have very little to do with reality; they're just isolated moments we should be grateful for, but not get addicted to.

It might seem perverse and illogical to you, but the Diana who came home and took off her make-up and kicked off her shoes didn't *want* to be followed, photographed and scrutinised any more. I wish the media wolf-packs had understood that, but they didn't. Whatever the location, whatever the time of day or night, to them I was fair game. "You can't want it one minute — and say, 'Get your hands off me!' the next," they all said.

Now where have we heard *that* one before?

5

Truth? Whose truth?

*The Truth is what has actually happened everywhere, and
when and where it happened, and why.
No-one can possibly know all that!*

I AM ABOUT TO lose a lot more friends now, but I'm sorry, it can't be helped. As far as I'm concerned, it's time some of the biggest and most persistently repeated lies were exposed. And there's no way of doing that without offending the liars themselves *and* everyone, everywhere who has swallowed their tainted merchandise whole.

Here it is:

The real history of this planet has never been told. In fact, it has been suppressed. The world's so-called 'holy' books are collections of teachings that were created to give comfort and reassurance to the people of their time, and to provide a suitable focus for their emotional and spiritual lives. And this they have certainly done.

But it has to be said, they have also been used as means of controlling and confining the faithful, rather than enlightening them. Dogma was designed to *prevent* us from thinking for ourselves.

They've been telling us for centuries that the scriptures are 'the word of God', and nothing but the word of God. Yet the painful truth is that most of them have been tampered with.

21

The Almighty did *not* authorise or transmit all of these 'holy' books. Some parts of them were indeed inspired, but others were later revised by priests and other hierarchies, who have used them to tighten their grip on their followers.

"So why didn't God intervene long, long ago, and put an end to this wholesale physical, emotional and spiritual slavery?" you ask.

Because in His/Her/Its wisdom, it had decreed that all those inhabiting the Creation shall have free will – without which, needless to say, we would all be puppets.

Fair enough. That makes a lot of sense. Except for one thing: right from the start, the Creator's more ambitious and power-hungry offspring have been using this prime directive – free will for all – as an excuse to carve their way through the galaxies more or less unchallenged, building empires and colonising suitable planets.

"I knew it! She's off her rocker! " I hear some of you cry. "The girl's finally cracked!" "What a load of rubbish! Pure science fiction!"

Well, if you prefer to go on believing a comfortable lie than to face an unpalatable truth, there's nothing I or anyone can do about it. But don't say I haven't warned you – before long the whole world will have proof of all of it.

In the last few thousand years, countless millions of innocent people have been murdered in the name of 'religion'. By whose authority? Not by God's. God is the *creator* of life, not the destroyer!

Men take each other's lives.

Men torture and punish each other.

Men nurse their hatred and resentment for centuries.

Not God.

So please – don't try and blame God for your *own* violence and cruelty – that's adding insult to injury, if you ask me.

Let's face it, despite all the skill, ingenuity and genius of the world's greatest inventors, architects, engineers and scientists –

and despite the courage and staying power of the human race – the great experiment called 'life on Earth' has run off the rails, and urgently needs a make-over.

In a world where free will is law, the powerful, greedy, cruel and corrupt are always going to grab the lion's share of whatever's on offer. It's simply not in the nature of kind, generous, honest and compassionate people to go around stealing and killing and enforcing their will.

And that is the biggest flaw in the plan, as I see it: *"Blessed are the meek, for they shall be repeatedly ripped off."* Or worse . . .

To my mind, one of the biggest challenges – no, not 'one of' – *the* biggest challenge facing mankind *and* the powers-that-be 'up here' who oversee human life, is to wipe the blackboard clean and come up with another plan altogether. One in which we all get the chance to evolve as individuals and as a civilisation *without* being controlled, conditioned and manipulated all the time – which is what has been happening on Earth for thousands and thousands of years.

Time to wake up

A sunny, late-summer afternoon. Diana and I are sitting on the grass, by a small stream. She has brought grapes and some apples, in case we get hungry.

She looks distressed.

Not wanting to intrude on her reverie, I say nothing.

"I was just thinking how sad it is that we all spend our lives searching for the truth out there," – she indicates the horizon, then gazes up at the sky – "or up there. We read books, we consult experts – and we allow people with their own hidden agenda to persuade us that there are no such things as other Universes and other realities."

She sighs, and slowly shakes her head.

"Yet all the time, we're perfectly equipped to find the answers *ourselves*," she goes on. She begins to count out on her fingers. "We've got our intuition, our imagination, our memory. We've got our unconscious, which can be woken at any time, if only we know how – but which *they* have been deliberately manipulating since the beginning . . . And, maybe most important of all, we've got our dreams. I'm sure dreams have been given to us as a kind of route-map we can consult when we lose our way."

I nod in sympathy.

"But most people have their receivers switched off, and their minds switched off," she continues, "so they never hear any incoming messages, and disregard their dreams."

"It's not our fault," I say. "We've been *programmed* to switch off – and to stay switched off."

"By whom, I wonder?" Diana replies.

Then she snaps out of it, picks up two apples, tosses one of them to me. "Oh well, not much longer now, and boy! is everyone going to wake up – and stay awake, this time!"

I nod again, and smile, and we sit for a while in the amber sunlight, contentedly chewing our apples. And then I wake.

6

A reminder

Have you ever wondered who owns Earth?
It's a prime hunk of real estate. Do you think it
would go ownerless in Space?! Skirmishes took place
and, approximately 300,000 years ago, certain
creator 'gods' came in and took over.

Barbara Marciniak
Bringers Of The Dawn

I T HAS OFTEN been said — by those who know — that it's better *not* to resist, challenge or oppose evil, but to accept it. Which is probably true — except when that becomes an excuse for sitting back and doing nothing to prevent it from doing any more damage than it already has.

Make no mistake, the poisoning of our minds and our planet has been deliberate. For reasons best known to themselves, certain groups have made every attempt to possess this world and control the people living on it — and during the last century, they came frighteningly close to achieving their aim.

But now the fightback has begun. This is the reckoning, the moment of truth. It's 'grown-up time', as they say — the time when we've got to take a deep breath and stop letting 'them' rule our lives and shape our destinies — whoever or whatever 'they' might be. It's time we stood on our own two feet, and stopped clutching the skirts of our spiritual elders and betters, so-called, like frightened children.

Our job in this Universe is to be co-creators with God — *not* sinners, grovelling at the feet of a bunch of unscrupulous overlords who use every trick in the book — lies, threats, blackmail, intimidation and, when all else fails, force — to keep us down.

The keynote of the Age that is now ending (approximately the last 2000 years) was devotion, which is a very beautiful thing — *unless* it means surrendering our dignity and self-respect to others, however exalted they may be — or may pretend to be. The keynote of the coming age is self-reliance. Which means we throw away the rulebooks others have written for us, and write our own.

So if someone tells you that their system is "the only Way" — run a mile. There are as many paths leading to the truth as there are human beings.

And probably a whole lot more besides . . .

7

Out of this world

THE NUMBER ONE question, of course, is, "What is heaven like?" It's not an easy one to answer, either, because it's different for everyone. But I'll try.

There isn't just one heaven, of course, there are hundreds of them – thousands, probably – each providing one 'note' or semi-tone in the 'great Octave' of Creation. And I have only visited two or three since I've been back. And the further 'up' you go, the harder it is to describe them, because nothing seems to be solid up there – you don't meet people, you find yourself flying through an ocean of energies and colours and thoughts and music. I say 'flying' because it's effortless – unlike swimming, which takes conscious effort; and I use the word 'ocean' because you're in it, and it's all around you.

Where I now live is what most people would think of as a paradise. If I want company, it's there; if I want to be alone, I am; if I want to be at home, I am; if I want to be out and about, exploring, I am. Everything happens at the speed of thought. There are no obstacles here, no delays, and no disappointments either. You don't need food, but if you want your favourite meal, you can have it – and you don't have to cook it unless you want to! (That's why they call it 'heaven'!)

There's no tiredness here, or illness, or weight problems, or disease. We still have bodies, of course, and when old people return here after their Earth lives are over, they gradually return to their prime. And when children arrive, they grow older gradually until they, too, are in their prime.

I'd now like to answer a few of the other questions I have been asked about life 'on the other side', so here goes.

Can you tell us what happened after you 'died'?
When I came to, it felt as if there was a ton weight lying on my chest. At first, I thought it was the car. But I quickly realised that it couldn't be – we were no longer in that tunnel, and the car was gone. We were in a room – no, not a room, a space without walls, filled with gentle, soothing light that seemed to be changing colour every few seconds.

Yes, there were a few people around – doctors and nurses, I suppose – but I'm positive it was the light and colour that were doing all the healing, rather than the people around us.

And the music! Yes, it's so obvious now – the music was healing us too! Nothing like the kind you hear on Earth – it wasn't classical or modern or pop – it was music that holds you like someone who loves you more than you've ever been loved before; that makes you want to laugh and cry at the same time. Music you never want to stop. But it did stop. And when it did, we were better again . . .

Did you suffer any after-effects?
Although we were better, I still kept feeling this heavy weight on my chest, as though something still hadn't mended properly. It went on for what I thought was two or three weeks – but turned out to be several months, in Earth time.

I spoke to a friend about it, and he told me what it was – and where it was coming from, so many of you were still thinking of me that I was being held in a powerful 'tractor beam', like the one the USS *Enterprise* had in *Star Trek*, which could capture other ships or tow them to safety if they were crippled.

Please don't think I'm not grateful for all the thought and prayer you sent my way. I'll never be able to repay you – and I'm not sure I deserved it in the first place.

Anyway, I got in touch with a friend in London — I knew she'd know what to do — and a day or so later I was free of that 'tractor beam'.

It can't be easy being famous. On Earth, celebrities have to lock themselves away from the public because so many people want to see them. Is it the same 'up there'? I mean, millions of people must still want to see Marilyn, or Elvis, or JFK, or John Lennon — or you.

Good question! And in a way, the answer is, "Yes." Except that we don't have to "lock ourselves away", because only our friends and loved ones know where we are! So there are no such things as intruders, obsessive fans, stalkers — *or* reporters or press photographers — I'm glad to say! But we *can* meet our friends, or groups of people, or attend concerts and events, whenever we like. And we do. And no-one ever hustles us.

Fame?

I wouldn't wish it on anyone — even my worst enemy, if there is such a person. As Marilyn once said, as she looked back on her career, "You wanna get there — and when you get there, what's there?" Fame is like being thrown into a furnace: once you're in, you can never get out. And even if your fame fades, you've still got problems — the furnace goes cold and you're a small pile of grey ash, forgotten by everyone.

But I needed mine. I can see that now. I *had* to become famous, to do what I wanted to do. I needed a platform. Becoming a Princess was the perfect platform — despite all the drawbacks. So you see, just as they used *me* — to produce an heir to the Throne — I used *them*, to give me the status I needed to do my work. Maybe that's why the alliance couldn't work — it was a marriage of convenience rather than of mutual love . . .

A lot of people are very ill when they 'die', or they have broken hearts or tortured minds, or they were murdered, or killed in wars or accidents. Are we all healed when we 'get home'?

Don't worry – however ill or damaged you are when you get here, you'll find yourself in the most wonderful 'field hospital' imaginable. Your pain – whether it's physical, mental or emotional – will be removed at once, and you'll be thoroughly rested and rebalanced.

The healing methods here are sensational. There are no surgical operations, anaesthetics or drugs of any kind. There's no pain. And there's no such thing as time here, either – what a relief it is not to be bullied by clocks and watches any more!

If you want to rest for an eternity, after a really difficult life, there's nothing to stop you doing so. And when you're fully recovered, you'll suddenly find yourself in your new home, being visited by friends and loved ones . . .

When we get to heaven, who lives with us? Do we have to live among people who have nothing in common with us, or are alien to us, or dislike us? Or are we surrounded only by people we're comfortable with?
On Earth, we're all thrown together – often with disastrous results – but up here, thank goodness, there's a separate world or dimension for people on the same 'wavelength'. Which means there's very little conflict or pressure or tension. You'll find yourself surrounded by all the people you *want* to be with – and who want to be with you.

Maybe that's why you-know-who had the idea of creating a parallel Universe based on duality – everything was too perfect in Paradise!

If there was only one kind of food, you'd soon get sick of it, however delicious it was – wouldn't you? If we get too comfortable, too rich or too successful, we can become complacent, or conceited, or both; but problems and obstacles give us the chance to test our character, determination, ingenuity, talent, courage, strength – you name it.

After we've settled in, do we review our recent life on Earth?

Yes. It's a very private thing — there are no judges, juries, magistrates or prosecutors present, you'll be glad to hear! You watch a replay of every significant action, thought and emotion you ever experienced, and you feel the full impact of it again — not only on you, but on the other people involved.

Believe me, it's a *very* sobering experience watching yourself make mistake after mistake after mistake — knowing you'll eventually have to get it all sorted. But there are consolations too — seeing how many times you helped someone, or did something unselfish, which had repercussions you only now get to see.

I said there were no judges or jury present, but that isn't strictly true. *We* are the judge and jury as we watch the action-replay of the highlights of our life. And a lot of people are very tough on themselves when they see how badly they screwed up, how many terrible decisions and choices they made. Believe me, I know — I'm one of them!

The name of the game is simply to face the truth — the good with the other stuff . . .

A lot of actors say they never read the reviews of their films and plays, or media gossip about their private lives. Did you read what your critics were saying about you? And if so, did it hurt?
Listen, I'm no angel — I made a lot of mistakes, and some terrible decisions too. When the flak was really flying, I could get mean and spiteful — and want revenge on my enemies too. I had no idea just *how* famous I was going to become, and that everything I did and said would be magnified so much, and scrutinised so closely.

Yes, of course some of the things they said hurt! One or two critics in particular kept banging on about my lack of education. No education yet devised could have prepared me for what happened when I stepped onto the public stage!

And no amount of university degrees and other academic achievements would have helped much, once I really got into my stride.

31

They kept on saying – they're still saying – that I lacked intellect. Well I'm no scientist or scholar, nor am I a philosopher or inventor, so I don't *need* a vast intellect! I *had* to be ordinary, and not some awesome intellectual – that's the whole point!

And anyway, what these people don't seem to realise is that all Creation is one vast ocean of thought, or mind, and *anyone* can tap into it for information, ideas and inspiration, at any time. Mozart knew – he used to say, "God knows where the music keeps coming from – but it keeps coming – sometimes so fast that I can't even write it down . . ."

'*In*sight.' '*In*formation.' '*In*stinct.' '*In*tuition.' '*In*tellect.' Have you noticed? They're all coming *in* from somewhere! The word 'invent' literally *means* 'come in'! Okay – so where are they all coming *from*?!

Where do you think the great ideas, systems, symphonies, buildings and technologies came from? From the human brain?! No, the human brain *processes* them once it receives them from the universal databanks.

I am not saying that certain men and women aren't geniuses – they most certainly are. It's the brilliant, intuitive way they reach out for vital new concepts then assemble the incoming data that makes them what they are – pathfinders, pioneers, innovators, inventors, leading us forward into a better world.

What I tapped into wasn't particularly new or revolutionary. I just started doing what most people want to do, in their heart of hearts – so suddenly everybody sat up and began to take notice. That's why I became so famous, even though I had nothing particularly original to offer – I was simply saying what almost everyone is thinking:

"Does it *have* to be so painful down here? Isn't there another way?" And even that was enough to get me into very hot water indeed, as you know!

Can you visit people on 'higher' and 'lower' planes than your own?
Yes. One of the most remarkable things I have noticed here is that when you're visited by someone from a higher level — or when they invite you to visit *them* — just being in their presence (being inside their energy field for a while) automatically 'raises' you to their level for as long as you're with them — which means that any differences of seniority or status between you immediately vanish!

As you might expect, 'seniority' and 'status' here have nothing to do with our social or professional standing on Earth — which no longer applies, of course — but with our spiritual rank, our character and our own personal vibration or aura.

Luckily, the reverse doesn't apply. If you visit someone who's still living in the semi-darkness, you might feel sad that they and the other people there have chosen to live there, but as soon as you're back home, there are no serious after-effects.

Occasionally we visit these levels because word has come through that someone there really wants to start returning to the light; and believe me, *nothing* can compare with the feeling of watching someone say goodbye to the shadowlands forever . . .

Why are some prayers answered, and others not?
Think about it for a moment. If all prayers were answered, and all wishes were granted, there'd be chaos — people would be asking for the most outrageous things. Imagine what would happen if the following prayers were immediately granted:

"Please may so-and-so fall madly in love with me, and have a sudden, uncontrollable desire for my body."
"Please may I win the Lottery."
"Please may those noisy slobs next door suddenly find themselves in the Arctic in their underwear."
"Please may my team win every match they play."
"Please may I have anything and anyone I want."
I'm sure you get the picture . . .

But here's a big surprise: although there isn't an army of recept-ionists sitting at a vast switchboard up here, there *is* the most amazing communications HQ, which receives and records not only all the prayers, but *all the thoughts and emotions of the entire human race, day and night*!

It's a kind of super-computer, and if I tell you what drives it, you'll think I have finally flipped. (But I haven't — honest!) It doesn't run on electricity, and it has no components or parts, like Earth computers. It runs on *thought*. In fact, the computer itself *is* a living thought — one that has been designed and given shape and a very specific purpose.

And who thought it up? Yes, you've guessed — our old friend, the Generator Of Dimensions: God. Right?!

Don't ask me how, but this machine — I don't know what else to call it — stores all incoming energy and *recycles* it, so that none of it is wasted.

So even if your (genuine, unselfish, constructive) prayers aren't answered, you can be sure that somehow, someone, somewhere is getting the benefit of them.

What happens when a man and woman 'up there' want to have a child?
Well as you'd expect, there's no need for sexual intercourse — the child isn't carried in the woman's womb, as it is on Earth. You'll be delighted to know that the child has some say in the matter, too! Which often isn't the case in the physical world, where a child can be conceived simply by a single sexual act, with or without any love being involved, or a conscious decision by the parents to try for a child. Up here, a child is the result not of a physical act (how could it be? we're not physical here) but of the mental, emotional and spiritual union of a man and woman.

And if there's a spirit somewhere that not only 'matches' the child that the man and woman are creating with their minds, but wants to share their life and experiences, they'll suddenly find that there are now three of them, not just the two.

The responsibility and the commitment must be total. You can't decide to have a child, then get bored with it after a while and change your mind – the way people sometimes do on Earth, and then abandon their babies. (And animals.)

And if the man and woman aren't intended to have a child – these things are dealt with at soul level, a few floors up – they simply won't have one. It's all a matter of compatibility and timing, and not of fertility . . .

Will there ever be peace on Earth?
As you know, there are people who have a vested interest in war. War is big business, and the profits are huge. But if enough of us keep sending out thoughts and prayers for peace, *nothing can stop peace from coming.* That's how powerful human thought is. It can even put the most colossal war machines out of business. Difficult to believe? Well here's a perfect example: Winston Churchill had a secret adviser throughout Word War II. Yes, a magician!

When things were going really badly for Britain – it hadn't prepared for war the way Germany had, and its armed forces, especially the RAF, were heavily outnumbered by the German forces – this man advised Churchill to introduce 'the Silent Minute'.

At 9 o'clock each evening, before the news was broadcast, one minute's radio silence was observed, so that listeners throughout the British Isles could focus their thoughts on victory and peace. Hitler, who knew how much power can be generated if millions of people meditate or pray together, was furious. He called it "England's secret weapon". And he was right – it *was*.

Are we all connected in some way? And are we responsible for each other?
We're all passengers on the same spaceship, or to put it another way, all fish swimming in the same sea. You probably know that whales, dolphins and sharks can pick up signals from their kind, and from other sea creatures, from miles away.

Well, in *our* sea, every thought and emotion we give out reaches *everyone else* in the ocean, however faintly — and every thought and emotion that *they* give out reaches us.

So we're all connected, quite literally, just as our spiritual teachers have been trying to tell us all along — but we haven't really believed them.

Like it or not, we *are* all wired into the same circuit — regardless of our age, background, race, culture, beliefs, intellect — everything. Your joy is my joy, your pain is my pain. *And however hard we try to lock each other out, we can't.* We're all in this thing together, kid! And the sooner everyone begins to realise it, the better.

Mahatma Gandhi once said that if we want to change the world, we must start with ourselves.
That's right, he did. And it wasn't just an airy-fairy piece of wishful thinking, it was a precise statement of fact, a scientific observation.

The buck *does* stop here — at home, with each one of us. We *all* have to make a big effort to start thinking kindly and compassionately — or at the very least tolerantly — about 'everyone else out there'.

And if we can somehow manage to do that, if we can stay with the programme, despite all the mud they sling at us for being so soppy — "Wake up, kiddo! Real life isn't like that! Real life's a bitch, every single day — and if you're not prepared to fight, you're finished!" — the turnaround will begin.

When enough people start thinking kindly of the rest of humanity — and it's looking pretty good already: you'd be surprised how many people are already on the case — at a certain point we'll reach flashpoint, and suddenly there *will* be peace on Earth, for the first time in recorded history.

And if a few demented warlords decide to push the button anyway, they'll find their weapon systems suddenly aren't working any more.

That isn't a threat, by the way — *it's a promise.*

I have been told by the top brass up here that if anyone *does* press the Armageddon button — instead of instant global destruction, there's going to be instant revelation . . .

Is there such a thing as hell?
Just as there are man-made hells on Earth, there are man-made hells up here too.

No-one is ever 'sent down' to these levels as a punishment: we all gravitate — or levitate! — naturally to our own level. But the moment anyone gets tired of life in the dark, and genuinely wants to return to the light, their rehab begins. And it's all done without any recrimination, guilt or humiliation.

Do animals go to heaven?
Of course they do. Anyone who has ever loved a dog or cat or horse, and looked deeply into its eyes, *knows* that they have souls, just as we do. One of the most wonderful surprises waiting for you when you get back home is meeting the animals you thought you had lost.

Are fairies, elves, pixies, gnomes, salamanders, water nymphs and their kind real — or do we just imagine them?
Of course they are! What an arrogant question! [*She giggles.*] Sorry, I didn't mean to be rude!

They were around *long* before we arrived on the scene. And they do a far better job of looking after the planet than we do! They don't create and invent the way we do — but they're far less destructive. They don't rationalise like we do — they're almost entirely instinctive, intuitive. And they've been incredibly patient with us — even though we test their patience to breaking-point, the way we rampage around, digging things up and chopping things down wherever we go . . .

What will happen to your 'Diana' self, if and when you decide to reincarnate?

Oh no, you're not seriously suggesting . . . ?! Not just yet, *please*! [*She laughs.*] No, really, I need a bit more time – not that there's any such thing as time here, of course – to get over the last lot. And to do some exploring up here.

But eventually, I expect I'll start thinking about what I need to do next – I have so much to learn, and quite a lot of personal stuff to sort out for myself – so I expect my guides and advisers will start turning up at odd moments, and eventually we'll get down to some serious discussions about what my next assignment should be.

And when the time and place and parents have been sorted out, 'Diana' will finally withdraw, and soon afterwards a baby will be born somewhere, who will have no conscious memory of having been 'Diana' at all – and her new life will give her – or him! (I might decide to be a man, next time round) – lots of opportunities to learn new things and do some work in a number of problem areas I left unresolved as 'Diana'.

But I'm told that if there's a need for 'Diana' to appear, to attend some conference or whatever up here, 'she' *will* appear – even though I have reincarnated! Does that make sense? It takes a while to get used to the mechanics of all this . . .

Is there really such a thing as karma?
Of course there is. What goes round *does* come round – it's the law of action and reaction, the law of 'inevitable consequence'.

And because duality seems to be the order of the day in the physical Universe – day/night, light/dark, weak/strong, and so on, our days of happiness and success are *always* offset by days of pain, drama and disappointment .

No-one is exempt. Behind the faces of even the richest, most famous, beautiful and distinguished public figures are hidden traumas and tragedies.

Were you by any chance thinking of the Queen when you said that?
Among other people, yes. Obviously, the Queen would give

anything to have had a life *without* all the shocks, scandals and unpleasant surprises she has had to put up with during the last fifty years, many of them involving her own family – *and* her in-laws, of course, myself included. [*Guilty as charged, ma'am!*]

As I see it, the greatest tragedy in the Queen's life is that she was trained – and willingly chose – to submerge her true self and always to be seen to be perfect, professional, dignified, distant, *royal*.

That was the price, her advisers kept telling her, that she must pay for keeping the ship of State on an even keel, as it ploughed through the stormy seas of the last half-century. But if only you could see the private person I was privileged to know for several years – witty, wise, playful, humorous, wonderfully sarcastic in a commonsense rather than a cruel way; informal, motherly, compassionate, *human*.

Oh, and while we're talking about the conflict between order (stability, continuity and tradition – everything the Queen stands for) and chaos (the hectic pace of modern life, and the inevitability of change) isn't it amazing that even physicists and astronomers are now talking about the 'dark energy' that seems to be driving the expansion of the physical Universe!

Maybe that explains the uneasy relationship between the two: no-one is talking about 'good guys' and 'bad guys' any more – but about two impersonal forces, one whose motto seems to be, "Why change things? They're fine as they are," and the other, which can't keep still, even for a moment.

What are your thoughts on the media?
One of the greatest inventions of the twentieth, or any other century. (I bet that surprised you!) At their best, they're the truth-tellers, the information providers. At their worst? They hunt like wolves – in packs, without mercy, and it's blood they're after, not truth.

I'd like to say a word to my friends in Hollywood, if that's okay, and to film and television companies in general: what *is* it with your obsession with hell and horror, ghouls and vampires and the so-called 'living dead'?! Come on, you guys, it's time you climbed out of there, scraped all that stuff off your shoes and took to the high ground.

Don't look now, but you're about to make one of the most astonishing – and profitable – discoveries you ever made. You're about to stumble on the one subject that just about *everyone* is interested in: what lies *beyond* physical life . . .

So what is *the purpose of physical life?*
You don't ask trivial questions, do you?! As far as I can make out, our job – you, me, all of us – is to undergo every conceivable kind of experience as we head for home, and to hand in all those experiences when we get there.

Everything we've ever done and said and thought and learned and achieved is entered into the planetary databank, and added to the sum total of human experience.

And in return?
We get our long-awaited, hard-earned, privileged backstage pass! And when – after many, many lifetimes – we finally step out onto that stage, we discard our personality forever – and for a brief moment *become* the star performer, the main event, the music, the audience, the applause, the auditorium, sky, sun, moon, the constellations and the galaxies themselves. And when all *that* has happened we simply, laughingly, lovingly, deliriously become one with all Creation . . .

*

There is a short silence. I try to swallow, but my throat is dry. Then she giggles. A second, shorter silence follows – then I hear a final whisper:
"I don't know about *you*, but I can hardly wait. Can you?!"

8

Final call

*You have come onto this planet with a coded
blueprint to carry light and to bring about a huge
planetary transformation. You have come to be the
standard bearer of your soul. You have been in
training for this assignment for lifetimes,
and you did not come unprepared.*

Barbara Marciniak
Bringers Of The Dawn

SOME OF YOU might have been shocked by my outburst a little
earlier. "That's not very ladylike," you might have thought. "And
not too dignified, either."

I'm sorry, but I reckon it's a little too late for ladylike and
dignified. This thing has gone on far too long, and far too far. A
handful of people – sinister, faceless men, hidden away behind the
scenes – have been ruthlessly manipulating human life ever since
Year One.

It doesn't really matter who or what they are, or where they
came from; the important thing is that they have been here all
along, playing with us like pawns on a huge chessboard. A war
wipes 10 or 15 million of us off the board? No problem – we breed
like rabbits, so there'll soon be another 15 or 20 million of us.

Occasionally, someone stands head and shoulders above the

crowd and starts suggesting that we *don't* have to keep on going to war and killing each other. Once again, no problem: they blow the trouble-maker away.

If you don't believe me, look in your history books. Just about everyone who dared to stand up and say there *has* to be another way has been murdered — either in secret, or in full view of the public.

But now, thanks to the media and the Internet, the genie is out of the bottle — almost everyone knows what is happening all round the world, as it happens. This increasing flow of information has given us all greater confidence — at long last the pawns are beginning to wake up, and to realise what's going on.

And when three or four billion people wake up, and discover that their entire lives are being cynically orchestrated — their beliefs, their education, their jobs, livelihood, food, health, prosperity (or otherwise) *and* their future too — the writing is well and truly on the wall.

Are you listening, gentlemen? Your little game is almost over. So be warned: by ruthlessly manipulating the entire human race, you have broken the Law on a truly epic scale — and by so doing you've run up some staggering karmic debts.

Maybe you think you're going to get away with it? Then think again. I'm not talking revenge or retribution here — the hundreds of millions of people you've tortured and murdered don't need to storm your citadels and tear you to pieces — even though they might be highly tempted to, when the truth emerges, as it will. The universal Law will not be mocked. *You* have devised your own reward, right down to the last detail. And nothing can undo it.

Maybe you're wondering what gives me the right to speak to you like this? Simple — the same right that every woman has. In case you guys hadn't noticed, we are the vehicles for birth and life. You? You are the destroyers, the torturers, the cynical, heartless manipulators, for whom a human life is worth about as much as a grain of sand or a speck of dust.

There are those who will argue that we're *all* playing roles in the great human drama – some of us have chosen to be heroes, others victims, still others bad guys – and that ultimately, physical existence is nothing but a dream or illusion, so no-one is to blame, however atrocious their behaviour, because the whole thing is a gigantic game.

If that's true, all I can say is that God must *enjoy* watching hundreds of millions of people being tortured and murdered – or, worse, he's totally indifferent, either way. But I'm not buying that particular version of the story. The designer/architect of the Universe and of Life itself and the extravagant beauty of Nature and the laws that uphold and maintain them couldn't possibly *also* be a bloodthirsty monster with an insatiable appetite for human blood and human sacrifice . . .

I could be wrong, of course – I often am! – but as I see it, whatever plan was drawn up in the beginning has run seriously off the rails, and now has to be put back on course. And even though we can't possibly all be responsible for this disaster, for some reason we have to put it right *ourselves* – we're stuck in the danger zone, so we can't sit back and expect God to make the first move. But the moment we get off our backsides and go for it, something tells me we *will* get the back-up so many of us have been praying for.

So how about we all roll up our sleeves *right now*, and get on with the job in hand?!

9

The greatest power of them all

No doubt about it, Man is a great inventor, creator and designer. The cities of the world, music, literature, science, technology, industry, monetary systems, education, aviation, telecommunications, medicine and who knows what else besides are the living proof of it.

But what of the world itself? And of the solar system? And of the atom? Who built *them*? Who created *all* the worlds, all the Universes? They certainly didn't happen by accident – they have a designer's fingerprints all over them. For thousands of years, some of the world's most brilliant scientists, writers, artists and explorers have been wrestling with this mystery. As have 'ordinary' people like you and me. And none of us has come up with definitive answers.

One of the biggest mysteries of all must surely be "What holds a galaxy, a solar system or a world in place?" If everything in the material Universe is made up of dancing atoms, with huge spaces in between them, what makes water hang together? What gives a flower – or a human being – its own particular shape and size, and stops it from falling apart and scattering to the four winds?!

How does a brick or a stone or metal maintain its shape and apparent solidity? And what is the law of gravity, so-called, that stops us from falling off the face of the Earth and floating away into Space?

Creating chaos is easy – any of us can do that. But creating *order*, creating an entire Universe in which not only every living and animate thing has freedom of thought and action, but also every substance, chemical, gas and element has its own integrity and its own vital role to play in the overall scheme is an absolutely mind-boggling enterprise.

I have thought and thought about it, and the best I can offer is this:

> The power that holds the atom together is – sorry, you
>   guys – love (the love/wisdom of the Creator).
> The power that holds a human being together is love.
> The power that holds a family together is love.
> The power that holds a community together is love.
> The power that holds a nation, a people together is love.
> The power that could hold humanity together, if only
>   it were given the chance, is love.
> The power that holds the world, the Solar system and
>   the Universe together is love.

Not the intense, emotional kind of love that attracts two people to each other – I'm not knocking it, mind you – I was looking for that kind for most of my life! – but a cooler, more dispassionate kind of love; love that is unconditional, makes no demands, has no expectations and is completely unselfish.

The tender love and concern of a mother or father. The love that only wants the *other* person to be well, to succeed and to be happy. In other words, the kind of love that lasts forever.

I am no scientist and no mathematician, but I can promise you this (and by the way, I have talked to the top brass up here, and you'll be glad to hear that they've given me the nod):

If we can all dump our own emotional luggage, all our grudges and hatreds, recent or long-standing, and go into love and forgiveness mode, *peace on Earth will come into being within 24 hours*!!! Yes, it's that simple. And what's more, we have the means to do it. To borrow a few words from Michael, if I may:

"It's World Referendum time, no less, and the choice we make now will decide the fate of the world. We are being asked to choose, and to work for, one of the two following parties:

the Dark   the Light"

10

Help is on the way

NOVEMBER, 2000. Lightning, thunder, rain, floods, rail crashes, wars; bad news being force-fed into three billion homes five times a day — a relentless diet of crime, murder, famine, disease and tragedy . . .

"I know, I know," she murmurs sympathetically. "Sometimes it's difficult even to get up in the morning, and wash and dress and get on with the day."

I manage a wan smile. Then remember my manners, and make a real effort to cheer up. (Come on, sourpuss, the lady could be sleigh-riding the Milky Way or boogieing with her best buddies up there somewhere — but she's chosen to drop in on *you*.)

"It does look pretty grim, whichever way you slice it," she goes on, "but believe me, help *is* on the way. From two completely different directions."

She has my full attention now.

"A lot of people are wondering if God has other things on his mind and has forgotten about Earth." She grins and shakes her head. "Uh-uh. We're very high on the list of His priorities — or Her priorities, if you prefer. In fact, right now, emergency moves are about to be made, behind the scenes."

"Sounds good," I reply. Understatement of the year, or should I say of the Millennium.

Diana smiles, then continues:

"They will activate circuits in all of us that have been lying dormant; open our hearts and minds to an entirely new range of ideas and possibilities; make it easy for us to chuck out all the old thinking that's harmful, irrelevant and obsolete — of which there's plenty!"

"Great news," I reply. "And the other direction?"

"The entire company of heaven, angelic and human beings throughout Creation, are answering the call. Their mission is to disperse the dark clouds surrounding the planet — which are the result of centuries of negative human thought and emotion, and the primal fear of the animals, who have always been hunted by other animals and by humans.

"It's these clouds that have been insulating the planet, preventing the human race from receiving the power and light being transmitted."

"And when is this going to happen?" I ask.

"It has already begun," she says. And then adds, by way of a goodbye: "Keep a grin — we're going to win."

She is gone as quickly and as quietly as she arrived.

We are fast approaching something:
Expect strange things to happen.
If you hold fast, what is about
to arrive will be good. It
is a gift. Go with it.
Hold your
vision
high, and
what comes
will be exactly
what the planet needs.

Peter Carbines
London, 15 July 1997

PART 2

Coronation

*Her life followed a dazzling
trajectory, such as the kind one
sometimes sees in the sky, from
the innocence of childhood to
Coronation, world celebrity, to
death in the absurd
carnage of an accident . . .*

M. Valéry Giscard d'Estaing
Former President of France

Forewarning

Saturday, 26 July 1997

I AM STANDING overlooking the ocean when I become aware of a youth – or could it be a girl? yes, it *is* a girl – suspended in the cloudless sky high above me.

Suddenly she descends head first, as if on an invisible bungee, which tests her physical, mental, emotional and spiritual endurance to the limit – almost disintegrates her; but she manages to stay in one piece. Just.

For a split-second her face is only inches away from mine – before the bungee pulls her abruptly up and away.

Another angle. I am looking inland, towards a mountain range set back from the coast. Now the girl plummets out of the sky towards these mountains. I expect an impact to occur, but instead, where she fell is . . .

Another planet in the sky, close to Earth.

Only the top half of this new planet is visible. It is blue/white, with distinct land masses and clouds, just like the Earth herself, and it takes up almost half of the horizon.

I wake up. Sensing – for do not dreams have their own authority? – that the girl's shocking fall is a signal that the longed-for moment has arrived.

The homeward journey is about to begin!

Aboard a renewed planet.

Postscript

Thirty-six days later, as news of a fatal car crash in Paris stunned the world, I realised the grim significance of this dream.

1

"A light has gone out across the world."

Anonymous card with flowers,
outside Buckingham Palace.

Sunday morning, 31 August 1997

I WAS JOLTED AWAKE by my bedside telephone. It was my old friend Simon Dee. His voice was clipped, staccato — he could have been a submarine commander in the conning tower, piping orders below for an immediate dive.

"Have you heard the news?"

Me, gathering my wits: "No. What?"

Simon: "Diana and Dodi are both dead. Killed in a car crash in Paris."

"Oh *no*!" This was my stunning, no-seat-belt introduction to a week that few of us will ever forget. Almost every television channel dropped its scheduled programmes and kept up an all-day electronic vigil. Shockwave after shockwave of emotion hit the public, the media, the embattled Royal family, the nation and much of the world. The miracle of the flowers began. Well-wishers flew into London from every direction. Virtually every other topic of news gave way to this one.

"And the country ached with sadness . . ."
ITV news reporter

Monday afternoon, 1st September

I went down to St James's Palace and was awed by the huge crowds, and the depth of their grief and dismay. There was a three-hour-long queue waiting patiently to sign the books of condolence; thousands of bouquets, cards, scribbled messages and lit candles lined the railings, brought by people from every walk of life and every continent. It was as if the place was under a palpable spell.

Churchill's State funeral and the shock and outrage of JFK's assassination came to mind; and the thought that in the last twenty-four hours the nation itself had begun to speak with an intensity that should give the Establishment occasion to engage in a little unflinching self-scrutiny.

On my way home I dropped into the Ritz Hotel in Piccadilly, and sat for a few moments in the Palm Court, to recover from the intense emotion of the crowds outside, and to pay my last respects to Michael Twomey, who had died a week or two before. For many years he presided over afternoon tea at the Ritz with warmth, friendliness, tact and quiet efficiency – and always found me a seat, however crowded it was.

I believe I was one of the very few men permitted to take tea there without a collar and tie: my Nehru jackets and Edwardian frock coat earned me privileged dispensation. Woe betide any VIPs and celebrities if they were collar-and-tieless: they were politely invited to take tea elsewhere.

Needless to say, my thoughts strayed to the Ritz in Paris, and its fateful role in the recent tragedy. One way and another, the day was crammed with intimations of immortality . . .

Here are just a few of the tributes that caught my eye outside St James's Palace, and in the newspapers, that day:

"Diana, you'll live on through *all* of us.
The whole country feels massively hurt without you."

Kim & Ashley

x x x

Card with flowers, outside St James's Palace

"Frailty, the apparent brave frailty of a candle in the wind, was
always Diana's supreme public quality in life. In death it will
combine with her other merits and faults – her genius for
intimacy, her great persisting beauty and her turbulent spirit
maimed in childhood – to perfect her legend . . ."

John Ezard
The Guardian

"She will reign forever as the
Queen of love."

Dame Barbara Cartland
An early prophecy, made years before

"Let them talk of a nation which threw away
a jewel bigger than its whole Empire."

Anonymous card with flowers, outside Kensington Palace

"Not even Shakespeare could have
crafted such a tragedy."

New York Post

"Your Royal Highness, it is like our heart has
been wrenched from us. With eternal love."

JM and Tom
Card with flowers, outside St James's Palace

"She's won, at terrible cost, the fight
for our unconditional love."

Peter McKay
Daily Mail

"The spirit of the age"

Christopher Hudson
Evening Standard

The Saviour spurned by the Court:
"Alone in the Royal Family, Diana saw that
the monarchy must adjust to survive.
Thwarted in life, she may yet succeed in death —
if Prince William continues her mission."

William Rees-Mogg
The Times

"Kings and Queens, princes and princesses are mirrors
in which we see ourselves and our times."

The Times
Monday, 1 September, 1997

"Born a Lady
Became a Princess
Died a Legend"

Tim & Ceri

Card with flowers, outside Buckingham Palace

I tucked my own offering into one of the bouquets lining the railings outside St James's Palace:

"Diana: Personal Envoy of the Goddess.
Many happy returns. Love, M."

Tuesday, 2nd September

A letter arrived from a good friend, Gwynneth Reed:

> Being in the prime of her life and health, the Princess will not need the long sleep some of us will. Without doubt she'll be much in command at her funeral, loving the spectacle of it all.
>
> I feel certain that this is the huge jolt the whole world needed, which will search the mind of every human being and lead to all we have been working for – you in particular, patiently waiting to be listened to, and no-one is listening.

Wednesday, 3rd September

No less than five friends called me, all of them sensing that Diana's mission is not yet complete – and that it is somehow connected with the vision that my creative partner Tony and I have had of the very near future. A very bold idea – but I ask you, could there *be* a better envoy than Diana? She always did want to be an Ambassador!

It is as if her death, shocking and deeply regrettable though it was, is part of the epic scenario now being played out on Earth. It has projected her legend into the stratosphere — *and* triggered a massive international response among 'ordinary' people who identified with "the fragile butterfly who changed our lives forever", as James Benson of the *Express on Sunday* has just described her.

Her suffering — as a child, later as a rejected wife, as an outcast of the Royal family and as a lonely exile in her own country — lit the fires in which her strength, her character and her mission were forged.

The symmetry, the balance is unmistakable: high aims and achievements can exact a terrible price.

"A light has gone out across the world"?

Yes, undeniably. But as my pal James sometimes says, *the reverse is also true*.

An even greater light has encircled the planet, dissolving barriers of race, creed and colour, and revealing the ideals we share, the world we are all yearning for.

"The Princess seemed to be in evidence everywhere, this afternoon."

Christopher Peacock
Commentating outside St James's Palace

"Do you think she'll be back? She still has very important work to do . . ."

Amanda Clark
During a telephone conversation

"The catalogue of royal blunders, oversights and
misjudgments continues to grow. Can *anyone*
still believe in 'a direct line of duty from
God to king to common man'?"

e-mail from a friend in Scotland

That evening, I wrote a letter to the Controller of Diana's household, suggesting that as the countless cards and personal messages lying with the flowers outside the three Royal palaces and other public buildings are a kind of national treasure, they should not be thrown away, but stored, later put into albums for public display, and a selection of them made into a book, to be published around the world, that would earn millions for Diana's Memorial Fund.

Rather than mail it, I decided to go down to Kensington Palace the next day, and deliver it in person. During the night I got up and made a large, bright pink heart and wrote on it in silver:

"Diana — this isn't the end:
this is just the beginning!
Thank you!
God bless.
Love from Michael."

"Perhaps no image, moving or still, said more about her — her
bravery, her restlessness, her sorrow — than those television
reports on the night of August 31, which showed the queen of all
our hearts and souls coming home at last, to RAF Northolt like
the good soldier she was. Her death has preserved her forever at
the height of her beauty, compassion and power."

Julie Burchill
News Of The World

"The truly Greek tragedy for Prince Charles is surely that, by
some Divine inspiration, he actually chose the Queen that the
nation – and, it appears, much of the world – wanted, but
through all-too-human passions and frailties, he could
not make it work."

Extract from a letter from a friend living in Wales

2

"She won't go quietly."

DURING HER NOTORIOUS *Panorama* interview on BBC television in November 1995, having unburdened herself of much of her pain and loneliness, and reviewed her ugly divorce from Prince Charles and the Royal family, a somewhat despondent and dispirited Diana suddenly – for the first and last time – referred to herself in the third person: "The trouble is, she knows what she wants. She won't go quietly."

It turned out to be a prophecy of devastating accuracy – and irony. (Echoing Ava Gardner's promise to Peter Evans, a few years earlier: "When I go, it won't be quietly – I'll send you a bolt of lightning." Which is precisely what she did – it felled a tree which all but destroyed his house in south London.)

Thursday, 4th September

After lunch, I took a train to High Street Kensington and handed my letter to a duty officer at the Palace gates. A huge crowd had gathered in the gardens nearby, and was milling around in the bright sunlight. Yesterday's atmosphere of shock and grief had given way to an almost festive air. By now, a wide river of flowers was overflowing from the Palace railings into the park.

I had the pink heart in my shoulder bag, and decided to attach it to a tree somewhere, rather than add it to the million – yes, million! – other tributes that had already arrived.

As I approached an isolated tree near the Round Pond, the image of Westminster Abbey's west door sprang into my mind.

"Yes, of course." I thought. "I'll go down to the Abbey tomorrow and ask if I can fix it to the railings."

I went home. A friend called, and I asked her where I should put the heart. She said, "You'll know. 'Upstairs' will tell you."

A moment or two later, the phone rang again. It was an old friend I hadn't seen or spoken to for a while, who happens to be married to a member of Diana's family.

"One ticket has become available for the funeral service on Saturday. Would you like to attend?"

Shock. Awe. Amazement. Disbelief. Profound gratitude.

And — how do I put this? — a curious feeling that this was not entirely a freak chance, but somehow part of a pattern. Only then did I remember that, three or four years before, Ellen Easton had suddenly said to me during a telephone conversation, "Your work in America won't begin just yet: first you have something to do here. It's connected with the Royal family."

I told Ellen it just didn't add up — I'd already *done* my bit for the Royals — passing on the warning about Prince Charles before his Investiture in 1969; sending him and Diana any of my writings that had to do with Britain and the future; writing letters of encouragement to Diana in her isolation — but she wouldn't budge:

"You've got something to do here first. And it involves *them*."

Friday, 5th September

I collected the ticket from my friend's house — it had been delivered by hand from the Lord Chamberlain's office at Buckingham Palace — said that I believe that Diana has set in motion a train of events that are virtually unstoppable, offered my tearful condolences and went on my way.

I decided to walk to Westminster Abbey, and work out a route through the crowds tomorrow, so I wouldn't be late for the service.

A few minutes later, outside a flower shop in Victoria, I was stopped in my tracks by a number of exquisite, formal flower arrangements destined to be laid outside the Abbey, later in the day:

"Light of the World, Princess of Peace."
— in Love and Gratitude —
**Stephen Anderson
& Layizha Malovich**

"To Diana — our Queen of Hearts
Gone but not forgotten.
Heaven is a lucky place today."
Mr and Mrs Proudfoot and family,
Scotland

"Arrivederci, meravigliosa Principessa."
Gli Amici di Rufina,
Firenze

"We love you so much."
Shirle, Andreas and Philipp
Altoner Strasse 5, 10557 Berlin

"God has taken his Angel home to rest."
Holly and Alison
New Zealand

63

The forecourt outside the Abbey's west door was packed solid. Press and television platforms were already in place and receiving a last-minute coat of royal blue paint. Behind barriers, hundreds of people had settled on the pavement with sleeping bags, cameras, food and votive candles.

A number of police officers were standing at the gates, and also an Abbey marshal. I asked him how guests were going to get through the crowds tomorrow, and not be late for the service.

"I have got to be here myself and open the Abbey, and even *I'm* not sure," he said affably.

He suggested I come to one of the nearest underground stations – Victoria, Westminster, Charing Cross or Embankment – and walk from there.

"If you get caught in the crowd, find a policeman, and he'll tell you where the next control point is, and so on."

I thanked him and moved off. Then remembered that I had the heart with me. I showed it to him, and asked if I could fix it to the railings, which by now were lined with flowers.

"Yes, of course," he said.

I looked up at the wrought iron gatepost itself. "I don't suppose I could . . . ?"

The nearest policeman nodded. "Yes, go on."

I climbed up and fixed the heart just below the pointed apex. A woman tugged at my coat and offered me a bunch of shocking pink roses, which I put beneath the heart.

I thanked the marshal, crossed the yard and looked back at the gates. The heart sang out against the grey stone of the Abbey behind it. Inwardly, I prayed that no-one would take it down overnight . . .

"To William and Harry, a small tribute
to your wonderful mother:
An Angel writing in a book of gold
wrote down Diana's birth
and ere he closed the book, he wrote
. . . 'Too beautiful for Earth' . . ."

Susan Cooper, Malcolm, Graeme, Leigh, Michael
Card with flowers, outside Westminster Abbey

"She has opened more hearts in one week than probably
any other human being in history. Her death, I believe,
is a perfect example of the Christ energy in action."

Gary
Somerset

That evening I called Ann Donaldson, widow of my late writing partner, Robert Donaldson, and told her where I'd be the next day. "You won't see me on television, but look out for the heart on the gate, when they all arrive at the Abbey."

Ann: "When I see the heart, I *will* be seeing you."

That's the kind of week it was: everyone finding something special to say to everyone else . . .

I switched on the television news.

Plans for Diana to be laid to rest in the Spencer family vault in the local parish church had been changed:

"Her brother, Earl Spencer, has announced that, in a break from a tradition going back for 21 generations, the Princess will be buried on a small island in a secluded lake in the grounds of Althorp Park. The ground has already been consecrated. In this magical setting," the news reader continued, with an eloquence that the week's events seemed to have inspired in everyone, "the dream will come to rest."

And, having rested awhile, the dream will awake once more. I have a hunch that, in the fullness of time, it is here, by a lake in the very heart of England, that Diana will hand her son his spiritual Sword of State. At his Coronation — should he accept his royal destiny — he will proudly wear his mother's mantle, woven from the love that people around the world had, and still have, and will always have for her. And so his own reign will begin. There is every indication that he will be a wise and gentle and intuitive monarch in a disunited kingdom which, as a parting gift, Diana briefly united.

In the small hours I went to bed, utterly exhausted after two nights with almost no sleep. But nothing, repeat nothing, could have prepared me for the extraordinary incident that was to occur, later that morning . . .

3

Goodbye, England's rose

From the adapted version of Candle in the Wind,
by Bernie Taupin and Elton John

Saturday, 6 September, 6 a.m.

I WOKE, SHOWERED, dressed in my best and took an early underground train to the Embankment. To my surprise, it was almost deserted. The Thames was still – not even a ripple on its surface. I sat for an hour overlooking the river. The sky was cloudless, and above County Hall the sun . . . the sun was literally twice as brilliant as I have ever seen it – and silver, not gold. Apparently, heaven itself had decided to turn it on a little, too.

No doubt about it – this was going to be a day of days.

8.30 a.m. I strolled down to Big Ben, where the crowds began, approached a group of policemen and asked one of them how I could get through to the Abbey, a quarter of a mile away. He asked if I had an invitation. I showed it to him.

"I'll have to escort you to the door, sir."

We made our way through a knot of pedestrians and mounted police and entered Parliament Square.

Only Orson Welles could have contrived what happened next,

it was so way, way over the top: a four- or five-minute uninter-
rupted tracking shot – the kind no other director would even
contemplate, it was so outrageous.

The square was packed with people, literally thousands of them
on either side of the road, waiting patiently behind the barriers
lining the pavements.

But the roadway itself was completely empty.

And so it was that in dazzling sunlight, and in utter silence –
broken only by whispers and the click of cameras as we passed (I
wanted to shout, "Save your film!" but after all, this was Diana's
day, and somehow she had contrived to make us *all* feel as if we had
a part to play in it) – my escort and I began our approach march to
the Abbey.

Left turn past the Palace of Westminster, containing both House
of Lords and House of Commons . . .

Outwardly I was relaxed, chatting to my escort, asking him
about the number of police on duty that morning – 24,000! –
telling him that what was happening to me right now was ten times
better than a knighthood, and so on. But inwardly I knew I had
entered a dream, and we were walking in slow motion, and the day
had a potent spell on it . . .

Right turn, past Westminster Hall and St Margaret's church . . .

Conspicuous privilege is a concept that has always made me
uneasy, and at that moment I desperately wished *everyone* could be
going to the Abbey. But hey, when the Universe goes to all that
trouble to cook up something really special for you, it would be
churlish to push the plate away. So I buried my misgivings and
began to enjoy my few minutes in the spotlight. Especially as the
spotlight was the sun itself!

Left turn into Broad Sanctuary, which runs the length of the
Abbey, past yet more silent crowds, and the hastily-constructed
media gantries . . .

And finally a left turn into the forecourt.

I thanked my escort and, as he withdrew, looked up at the gate.

The pink heart was still in place!

I got permission to put up two other cards I had made during the night. The first, an Arthur Rackham illustration I had found in *The Romance Of King Arthur*, showing a fair-haired maiden carrying the Holy Grail at the Castle of Corbin.

She is standing, head bowed, her body enveloped in sacred fire whose flames support her feet. The resemblance to Diana is uncanny. The second was a green shield on which I had written in silver:

"The whole world loves the Lady of the Lake."

Under the curious gaze of a hundred telescopic lenses and television cameras – no wonder the famous think of them in terms of wolf packs about to pounce – I made my way back to the great North Door, where the other guests were waiting for the Abbey to open.

Our tickets said, 'Non-Ceremonial Day Dress or Lounge Suit' – but no-one was listening. I have never seen such elegance in all my days. Tacitly, everyone had decided that Diana deserved the business, the very best, the full fig.

For my own part, I had decided to dress for a wedding, not a funeral – Edwardian frock coat, white silk scarf, diamond star and glittering acrylic heart, black patent leather boots.

Wedding?

Yes: the alchemical wedding of the Princess to her people – the countless millions around the world who are yearning for, praying for and working for a more compassionate society.

9.30 a.m. The North Door opened and we made our way slowly into the Transept. I was greeted at the entrance by Ken Lucraft, the friendly marshal who had allowed me to climb the west gate the day before, and shown to an aisle seat by a military usher. I could hardly believe my eyes. We were only a few rows behind the seats reserved for the Spencer family, facing the catafalque and directly opposite the South Lantern where the Royal family would soon be sitting.

On either side of us, incongruous among the statues of great statesmen of yesteryear, television monitors had been installed, which meant that we would miss nothing.

I looked to my left. And found that I was seated next to Elizabeth and David Emanuel, who created the fairytale wedding dress which had signalled the beginning of Diana's 'reign'. The symbolism was breath-taking. Queen Noor of Jordan arrived, followed by Mrs Hillary Clinton and other dignitaries. Then the Spencers. And finally the Royal family.

As the flower-decked coffin arrived in the sacrarium, borne by young Welsh Guardsmen, I closed my eyes – and received the distinct impression that the Angel of the Presence was in the Abbey, in order to preside over what was clearly not merely a State occasion, but one of even wider significance.

The ceremony itself – and the inescapable sense of history being made before our very eyes that underscored it – was almost too powerful to comprehend or describe.

The stoicism of the young Princes; the face of their father, bearing his all but intolerable burden of regrets; sublime music floating away into the arched roof; then, without warning, the startling moment when her brother, Earl Spencer, knight gallant and Keeper of the Flame, ablaze with righteous indignation, withdrew Excalibur from its scabbard and brought it down with devastating force:

"I stand before you today as the representative of a family in grief, in a country mourning, before a world in shock. We are all united, not only in our desire to pay our respects to Diana, but rather in our need to do so.

"For such was her extraordinary appeal that the tens of millions of people taking part in this service all over the world via television and radio who never actually met her, feel that they too lost someone close to them in the early hours of Sunday morning.

"It is a more remarkable tribute to Diana than I can ever hope to offer her today.

"Diana was the very essence of compassion, of duty, of style, of beauty. All over the world she was a symbol of selfless humanity. All over the world, a standard-bearer for the rights of the truly down-trodden; a very British girl who transcended nationality. Someone with a natural nobility, who was classless and who proved in the last year that she needed no royal title to continue to generate her particular brand of magic.

"Today is our chance to say, 'Thank you' for the way you brightened our lives, even though God granted you but half a life. We all feel cheated that you were taken from us so young, and yet we must learn to be grateful that you came along at all.

"Only now that you are gone do we truly appreciate what we are now without; and we want you to know that life without you is very, very difficult. We have all despaired at our loss over the past week, and only the strength of the message you gave us through your years of giving has afforded us the strength to move forward.

"There is a temptation to rush to canonise your memory. There is no need to do so. You stand tall enough as a human being of unique qualities not to need to be seen as a saint.

"Indeed, to sanctify your memory would be to miss out on the very core of your being, your wonderfully mischievous sense of humour, with a laugh that bent you double.

"Without your God-given sensitivity, we would be immersed in greater ignorance of the anguish of AIDS and HIV sufferers, the plight of the homeless, the isolation of lepers, the random destruction of land mines.

"Diana explained to me once that it was her innermost feelings of suffering that made it possible for her to connect with her constituency of the rejected.

"And here we come to another truth about her: for all the status, the glamour, the applause, Diana remained throughout a very insecure person at heart, almost childlike in her desire to do good for others, so she could release herself from deep feelings of unworthiness, of which her eating disorders were merely a symptom. The world sensed this part of her character and cherished her for her vulnerability, while admiring her for her honesty.

"The last time I saw Diana was on July 1st, her birthday, in London when, typically, she was not taking time to celebrate her special day with friends but was guest of honour at a special charity fund-raising evening . . .

"There is no doubt that she was looking for a new direction to her life at this time.

"She talked endlessly of getting away from England, mainly because of the treatment that she received at the hands of the newspapers. I don't think she ever understood why her genuinely good intentions were sneered at by the media – why there appeared to be a permanent quest on their behalf to bring her down.

"My own and only explanation is that genuine goodness is threatening to those at the opposite end of the moral spectrum. It is a point to remember that of all the ironies about Diana, perhaps the greatest was this: a girl given the name of the ancient goddess of hunting was, in the end, the most hunted person of the modern age.

"She would want us today to pledge ourselves to protect her beloved boys, William and Harry, from a similar fate, and I do this here, Diana, on your behalf:

"We will not allow them to suffer the anguish that used regularly to drive you to tearful despair. And beyond that, on behalf of your mother and sisters, I pledge that we, your blood family, will do all we can to continue the imaginative, loving way in which you were steering these two exceptional young men, so that their souls are not simply immersed in duty and tradition, but can sing openly as you planned.

"We fully respect the heritage into which they have both been born, and will always respect and encourage them in their royal role; but we, like you, recognise the need for them to experience as many different aspects of life as possible, to arm them spiritually and emotionally for the years ahead. I know you would have expected nothing less from us.

"William and Harry, we all care desperately for you today. We are all chewed up with sadness at the loss of a woman who was not even our mother. How great your suffering is, we cannot even imagine.

"I would like to end by thanking God for the small mercies He has shown us at this dreadful time: for taking Diana at her most beautiful and radiant, and when she had joy in her private life.

"Above all we give thanks for a woman I am so proud to be able to call my sister – the unique, the complex, the extraordinary and irreplaceable Diana, whose beauty, both internal and external, will never be extinguished from our minds."

As the spontaneous eruption of applause from the crowd outside poured through the open west door, advanced up the nave and flooded the entire building – the royal family and a few senior clerics were probably the only people not applauding – it occurred to me that, not since Spencer's kinsman, Winston Churchill, galvanised the entire nation half a lifetime ago, had anyone so incisively voiced the will and desire of so many of the people.

And what of Diana's solemn, processional departure from the Abbey, to a thrilling crescendo of alleluias from John Tavener's *Song for Athena*, whose startling dissonances poignantly echoed those in the Princess's own life?

I confess to a surge of pride that someone who, years ago, had been at the same school as myself, later became a man whose musical genius, like that of Verdi, Elgar, Albinoni and Bach, so unforgettably enriched the day.

"You shared your life with us; God give you eternal life.
You gave your time to us; God give you his Eternity.
You gave your love to us; God give you his unending love.
You gave your life to us; God shed on you
his perpetual Light."

BBC TV commentator **Tom Fleming**
as Diana left the Abbey for the last time.

"The soldiers are picking up Diana in the box."

John
Tollgate Primary School, Plaistow, London.
(a painting of the coffin and its pallbearers
on the railings of Westminster Abbey)

As I made my way back through the silent crowd in Parliament Square, it also occurred to me that, of all Diana's many achievements, none could be more unexpected than the way in which she has exploded forever the myth of the British people as inhibited and incapable of outward emotion.

And, apart from their grief, what must Steven Spielberg and Tom Cruise — who were in the Abbey with their wives — have been thinking about the majestic ceremony they had just attended?

"Got to hand it to you guys — you put all this together in *six days*?! It sure beats anything Hollywood could do, hands down."

"Princess Diana once memorably said that
she wanted to be queen in people's hearts.
Perhaps what we are seeing in the
streets of London today is the
Coronation of that Queen."

A bemused **David Dimbleby**,
senior BBC TV commentator,
as the cortège reached Hyde Park Corner
on its homeward journey.

"In mourning the death of the Princess,
all the people of Ireland will be united . . ."

Irish television newscaster.

"And this service in Westminster Abbey was carried
live on Egyptian television, where the Princess has been
referred to as the Cinderella of the century . . ."

David Dimbleby
As the cortège approached
the Regent's Park Mosque.

"Dina you was my only
hope Dina you was my only
love Dina you was kind.
I love you
god plase you in heven Dina

Lilian Blackbrun. Age 7
N Jer

*Card on the railings of Dorset Square,
Marylebone, which Diana's motorcade passed,
on its way home to Northamptonshire.*

"It's almost as if a people's wreath is
assembling itself on the hearse . . ."
David Dimbleby
*As the cortège passed the crowds in the
Finchley Road, shortly before it left London.*

"The men of my tribe never cry —
but they are crying today . . ."
An Aboriginal woman on Australian television.

The theory:

Today, the shadows are long because we have lost a light that shone brightly and gently. On behalf of the President and the American people, I came here to express our deep sadness at the loss of Princess Diana. We grieve for her children, her family, and her country. We can honour her memory by continuing her work; by bringing care and comfort to the afflicted; by reaching out to those who are stranded on the outskirts of hope and opportunity; by treating every child with love and compassion.

Hillary Clinton
*Speaking in the garden of the US Ambassador's
Regent's Park residence in London.*

The practice:

Congress approves $40 million to fight teens

Washington, DC. Taking a "zero tolerance" stance against the growing problem of young adulthood in the US, Congress approved legislation Monday allocating $40 million toward the fight against teens.

"As much as we all wish it would, the problem of teens is simply not going away in this country," Senator Frank Lautenberg (D-NJ) said. "In fact, it's growing. I'm pleased we're finally starting to devote some real money and resources to the problem."

Under the new legislation, any US citizen found to be between the ages of 12 and 20 can be jailed for up to two years for a first offence. So-called "serial teens" can be jailed for life.

e-mail from Washington DC, October 1997

"I've taken the children to people dying of Aids,
to homelessness projects . . . to all sorts of areas where
I'm not sure anyone of that age in this family
has been before. They have a knowledge –
the seed is there and I hope it will grow,
because knowledge is power."

Diana
speaking on BBC TV's Panorama, *1995*

Laurence Chambers, who suffers cerebral palsy after
being beaten as a baby, met the Princess when he was
chosen to show her round the Institute of Conductive
Education in Moseley, Birmingham, during the official
opening in October 1995.

As he led her back to her car, she bent to give him a
goodbye kiss. Laurence threw his arms round her
neckand responded with a lingering kiss and cuddle. "I
didn't let go, so she picked me up and gave me another
hug," says Laurence, giggling.

When the Institute received six tickets to attend her
State funeral, Laurence was a natural choice to travel to
London as the main representative with his dad.
"Afterwards we went to St James's Palace to lay some
flowers. I wrote on my card, "To Diana – I will
think of you and love you forever."

Christine Challand
A Tribute to the People's Princess
Sunday Mirror, *August 1998*

4

The local girl beloved of the world

Anthony Holden

From his book Diana: A Life and a Legacy

DIANA'S FUNERAL WAS ATTENDED, via television, by some 2.5 billion people around the world, getting on for a third of the world's population. In London, the route of the procession had been lengthened to accommodate the crowds, by public demand, and for fear that people might die in the crush to mourn her. Thousands slept out on the streets overnight, knowing that nothing like this would ever happen again in their lifetimes. There had been no comparable event in British history.

Only 2,000 mourners could be crammed into Westminster Abbey, but at least they included as many true friends, colleagues and beneficiaries of the dead Princess as the great and the good, who are usually allowed to hijack these occasions. Again, "people power" had won the day, ensuring that world leaders and European monarchs were less entitled to ex-officio seats than people who had actually known Diana, cared about her, loved her. Before the day was through, they were to become part of another unexpected, quite unprecedented display of the popular will.

Women wailed, in a very un-British way, as the coffin left Kensington Palace on its four-mile journey to the Abbey. As it passed Buckingham Palace the Queen, who bows to no-one, inclined her head towards her dead ex-daughter-in-law, the free spirit whose banishment from her family was now causing her such grief.

As the coffin passed St James's Palace, where it had lain all week, Diana's sons joined the procession to walk solemnly behind it, flanked by their father, uncle and grandfather. William could scarcely lift his head all the way, while young Harry braved his life's worst ordeal with astonishing composure.

After Diana's favourite passage from the Verdi *Requiem*, Elton John dragged the monarchy further towards the present day by singing a pop song, *Candle in the Wind*, his elegy for Marilyn Monroe, with new words specially written for his friend Diana. As its last tender strains died away, the applause from the crowd outside began.

Then Diana's brother Charles unleashed a tribute which turned into a tirade, against the media who had dogged his sister's life, and the royal family who had tried to reclaim her in death. Before the world, he pledged to his dead sister that her "blood family" would do all in its power to continue "the imaginative, loving way" in which she had been bringing up her sons, "so that their souls are not immersed by duty and tradition, but can sing openly as you planned".

As Charles Spencer's voice cracked with emotion, the applause outside began again. This time, despite the implied insult to the senior royals in the midst of the congregation, it invaded the ancient Abbey, starting at the back, then creeping down the sides until the entire church apart from the Windsors was clapping. Even poor William and Harry, blinded by grief and untrained in royal protocol, joined in.

It was the nearest the House of Windsor has yet come to face-to-face rejection, the moment it knew for sure that it must change to survive.

Diana was causing trouble again, even from within a stately

coffin draped in the royal standard. The wailing continued afterwards, as it was placed in the hearse for the eighty-mile drive to Althorp.

Crowds lined the entire route, right up the M1 motorway, throwing flowers in such profusion that the driver had to stop to clear the windscreen. By the time it reached her childhood home, its path strewn with floral tributes, the hearse's sombre black was garlanded in the bright colours of Nature.

The local girl beloved of the world was returning home for the last time. As she disappeared through the gates of the estate, offering the photographers the last pictures they would ever take of her, the curtain was drawn on one of the most remarkable days in modern British history.

The will of the people had opened up a seismic fault beneath the 1,000-year-old British monarchy, shaken to its foundations by the popular feeling for a free-spirited force of Nature, loved all the more by the people for her rejection by the royals.

She was buried on an island in a lake at the heart of the estate, which she had loved in childhood, and where her sons can now visit her in privacy whenever they want, while the rest of the world gains occasional access to pay its lasting homage. Within hours that island too was carpeted with flowers, hiding the scars in the earth which had finally quenched Diana's abundant spirit.

The royal family retreated to Balmoral that same evening, but it was to take days yet for Britain to return to anything remotely approaching normal. The signal, again by popular will, came four evenings later at Wembley, the national soccer stadium, when a vital World Cup qualifying match was preceded by a minute's silence for Diana. The 75,000 crowd wept again, cradling their candles against the wind, as Elton John's elegy echoed around the country one more time. But Elton himself had said that day that it was now "time for life to go on".

And the referee's whistle, by universal consent, signified the freedom to stop talking about Diana in hushed tones, and honour her memory with smiles, cheers and laughter. The England players, all wearing black armbands, dedicated their performance that night to her memory. They won 4-0.

As darkness fell eighty miles away, ten days after her death had convulsed the nation she loved, just who lay buried on that island? As it falls again tonight, who lies there now?

A beautiful young mother, cruelly cut off in her prime?

An incarnate idea whose time had come, inspiring Britain to cast off its post-imperial shackles and look to its European future?

A martyr to the media age? Or a saint in the making, who by her own example has turned us all into better people?

*

It is hard not notice that at 36, Diana has died at the same age as that other iconic blonde of the century, Marilyn Monroe. In that, there does seem to be something hideously inevitable about her early death, as if she was always going to become immortal in the way that only stars can.

There are plangent similarities between the two 20th century goddesses. Arthur Miller wrote of Marilyn Monroe that no-one had such a gift for life as she did, that she could come into a room and light it up, that her vitality transformed others. The same could be said of the late Princess, who so longed for the reciprocated warmth of others.

Nigella Lawson
The Times
September 1, 1997

5

Shielding the flame (i)

In its majesty and scale and aura, her funeral
will inevitably be compared with Churchill's.
But with Churchill, the funeral was a burial of something
already gone. Diana's death points
in exactly the opposite direction . . .

Andrew Sullivan
The Sunday Times

Sunday night, 7th September 1997, 11.30 p.m.

I SAT AT MY PC, dashed off the following e-mail and sent it to Peter Quiller:

Hi! I arrived home early this evening from a day in the country, and was dressing before returning to the Abbey to seek permission to remove my three cards (the heart, the Grail Maiden and the Lady of the Lake shield – as I think they'll eventually fetch a tidy sum at auction, to be donated to Diana's Memorial Fund) when the phone rang. It was John Prudhoe. He said, "We *must* get someone to seal the Abbey, to contain the immense power it received yesterday, and ensure that it doesn't drain away." I told John I was about to go there, and asked how it might be done. He said, "You'll be told." I took the sceptre stone with me (a copy of the *Star of Africa* diamond in the royal sceptre) and set off.

8.15 p.m. Last light. I arrived in Parliament Square. To the west, a hunter's moon hung in the sky behind the Abbey! I found my way to the West Door. The forecourt was still packed with people, drawn, no doubt, by the power of the momentous events of the previous day, which somehow still lingered in the air around us like a heavy perfume, or sound, or the aftershock of an earthquake.

> *"May the great Power that was received here yesterday be sealed, and used according to Your will, and not dissipate or drain away. Thank you. It is done."*

I opened my eyes. No-one was looking. (Don't think they could see me!) Repeated the procedure at the North Door and at the south and east walls. Once again, nobody took a blind bit of notice of the man in his black sharwani and white scarf, wielding what looks like a zonking great diamond. Opened my eyes again. The Abbey now seemed to be surrounded by a faint, luminous ring of fire!

I faced the Palace of Westminster, invoked that some of yesterday's Light and Love and Power be released into the House of Lords and the House of Commons. Stood beneath the epic statue of Winston Spencer Churchill (busy lot, these Spencers, aren't they?!) and thanked him for all *he* did; moved to the bottom of Whitehall, aimed the stone at the Cenotaph and thanked all those who gave their lives in two World Wars so that we might have yesterday and today.

Went home. Reported to John Prudhoe. Word-processed this. Am about to make toast and tea then totter off to bed. (*Please, please, you guys up there – no more dragging me out of bed at three or four in the morning!*)

Talking of being dragged out of bed, yes, it happened again last night: I was told, "Take a look at *The Dragon King*, kid." Crawled out of bed. Did so. Was blown out of my bedsocks. It matches the events of Saturday like you wouldn't – correction, like you *would!* – believe. There are so many parallels I literally gasped:

Merlin's speech at Westminster Hall, when he tells the assembly about Prince Arthur's years of training!! Arthur's Oath of Allegiance at his Coronation in Westminster Abbey!! It could be Prince William speaking!!

And Merlin's final affirmation about what is to come!! Dig up your copy of *The Dragon King* and blow your mind, pal. Looks as if it's time has finally come. Thanks, Diana!

I feel as if I've run up and down Ragged Stone hill six times in succession – non-stop. In full pack and rifle . . . I'm gone. No I'm not – one final item:

William Elmhirst called, and told me he and Heather were at Avebury, doing fieldwork – and simultaneously listening to Diana's funeral on the radio. The commentator homed in on the heart at the Abbey's west door and read out the inscription over the air. (*"Diana – this isn't the end: this is just the beginning!"* etc.) William said, "We *knew* it was you, Michael. We just knew . . . !" M. J

Diana, first lady of the global village
The triumph of magic over the message
*The Princess's life was a series of brilliant fictions
that turned into something quite extraordinary*

Bryan Appleyard
The Sunday Times

Down in the engine room of the culture she had, without anybody being fully aware of the fact, attained some sort of ultimate celebrity. She has become, as everybody keeps saying, 'an icon', like Elvis Presley, Marilyn Monroe, Evita. But there is more to it than that. Diana died everywhere and instantly – on the Internet, CNN and every television screen in the world, on the radio, in every newspaper. She was the first icon fully to live and die in the global village.

As such, she has become, arguably, the greatest celebrity ever. And celebrity is one of the most potent forms of contemporary magic. The over-the-topness, the irrational unexpectedness of the mourning is a sign of this potency. This week, we have been watching the triumph of magic.

But why Diana? Well, first there was the beauty. But this was not merely beauty, this was the beauty that leapt through the lenses. She seemed chemically bonded to film and to video. Her gestures – especially that initially shy dip of the head – were vivid enough to survive the technological transitions. She was what show-business people call a 'natural'.

Then there was her incredible story. She started out as the supreme royal. But then, as the fairy tale turned to soap opera, she became something more: a kind of one-woman rainbow coalition of every imaginable trauma from infidelity to marriage breakdown, from domestic humiliation to global conflict.

On the Internet the point becomes ever more graphic. Dozens, maybe hundreds, of new Websites for Diana have sprung up – some simply bearing a picture of flowers, others explicitly addressing her on the assumption that she sits next to Mary, at God's table. Both the electronic notices and the paper ones at the shrines pray for her intercession for the cure of disease and the relief of suffering. Just as in life she resurrected an ancient idea of royal magic that could cure by the laying on of hands so, in death, she has given expression to a basic form of religious fervour that most of us thought had vanished.

It would be easy but unwise to be contemptuous or condescending about this. Religious fervour may be seen as a marginal phenomenon in the world of late liberal capitalism. But its expression on this scale means something. At the most obvious level it means that Diana has become more than royal. She has subverted the ancient magic of monarchy with this new, more dynamic, more popular magic.

Yes, I was a cynic until I met her

Once, at a hospital in Huambo, when the photographers had all flown back to their air-conditioned hotel to wire their pictures, I watched Diana, who was unaware that any journalists were still present, sit and hold the hand of Helena Ussova, a seven-year-old who had had her intestines blown to pieces by a mine. For what seemed an age the pair just sat, no words needed. When Diana finally left, the small girl struggled through her pain to ask me if the beautiful lady was an angel. Could anybody have said no?

Christina Lamb
The Sunday Times

Monday, 8th September

As the tide of grief continued to rise – ankle-, knee-, waist-, chest- and throat-high, or so it seemed, with no sign of abating – I found myself wondering why no-one had mentioned the one person who must be suffering most of all: Princess Diana herself.

Everyone was sending out sympathy and concern to her two sons, and rightly so: they had just been dealt the cruellest, most sadistic public ordeal an unfeeling Providence could devise. These two brave young men had, and still have, every right to expect that outpouring of sympathy.

But what of *Diana's* grief? With brutal suddenness, she had been separated from the two people she loved most in all the world: her own sons – two companions, playmates who made all her pain and isolation bearable.

Yes, of course she can reach through to them when she wishes – and doubtless, being sensitive, both Harry and William often feel her presence with them; even hear her voice, her laugh. But how much she must wish to hug *them*, and not the tantalising hologram of them that appears to her whenever she homes in on them from beyond the veil . . .

A letter arrived, from Peter Quiller:

Last night I went out under the stars to ask the Guardians what was going on. First I asked whether Diana's death had been designed, planned, plotted or in any way orchestrated by her enemies. Then I asked if it had been an accident, pure and simple.

There was no response to either question. I began to frame a third question in my mind and started to voice it. A bright shooting star sped out of the Draco constellation – the King!

Here is what I had begun to ask: 'If there was no sinister sub-plot or subterfuge behind her death, and it wasn't just an accident, then was it some kind of divine plan?'

Of course, the answer was in the affirmative: as so many of us have suspected, it is what she incarnated for, and lived for. It was her divine mission all along, to provide the focus for a return to an awareness of the Goddess – the originator of everything, 'the Mother of the ten thousand things'.

And so, after such a long, long time – it begins!

Peter's letter came with a rather intriguing enclosure:

Today I consulted *The Celtic Tarot* about Diana's death, and its inner meaning. The card I drew was the Star. And this is what the Tarot had to say: "The Star is a card of hope, and a symbol of the universal beauty of Nature. The circular wheel is a symbol of the Earth in perfect harmony. The Dove of Peace is flying upwards, to signify the soaring spirit of Man. The pentacle touching the circle of the Universe is a five-pointed star and is associated with the five magic symbols of light and hope in Celtic mythology. They were recorded thus:

88

The living, fiery spear of Lugh; the magic ship of Manannan; the singing sword of Conery Mor; Cuchulain's sword which spoke; and the Lia Fail, Stone of Destiny.

Each one represented a divine aspect of God through which Man could rule on Earth. The figure of the naked lady clothed in the purple robe is carefully pouring the healing waters of Aquarius. The Aquarian vision is a progressive one, a reforming with humanitarian principles, a healing force in its highest form.

The Star is a radiantly beautiful concept of life . . . which symbolizes the Garden of Eden restored on Earth, a visionary concept of the new Age which could restore Man to his rightful place in the Universe.

On a more personal level, this card deals with restoring the hopes and faith of the querent, and opening up a new, as yet inconceivable horizon. It shows the world with a new ideal and meaning – a revolutionary ideal which requires a change of attitudes. It speaks to the individual as no other card can, indicating a time to seek one's destiny.

The Star is a shining light which brings hope, often in the hour of crisis where darkness seems to immobilise the senses.

*

Even in her estranged state, she continued to play a real royal role, drawing significance from the family and the institution which she never quite took as her own – and enhancing it.

Her determination to use her unique prominence for earnest ends, to use the glass of fashion to magnify the suffering of others, lent grace to the monarchy.

She helped to ensure that the public identified the monarchy with social purpose rather than simply Society. And, in affirming that specifically royal role, and in treating her membership of the institution as a vocation that did not end with her marriage, she communicated her own sense of the enduring importance of the Crown.

By her public action she showed that she was a true defender of the Throne that her son must one day inherit. That is how she deserves to be remembered. And that is how she must be remembered.

The Times
Leading article
September 1, 1997

6

Shielding the flame (ii)

A FEW NIGHTS LATER, it occurred to me that we had only sealed Westminster Abbey: the huge wave of energy generated by Diana's passing and now encircling the planet needed the same kind of attention. Clearly, we still had some work to do.

Next weekend I visited Peter Quiller, and beneath the giant oak in his garden, Peter, his wife Bran, their daughter Amanda, their son Tim and I carried out a short, informal ceremony – despite all the noise and distraction going on all around us: Peter's house is a tiny, once-unspoiled rural oasis surrounded by roads, housing estates, buildings sites, barking dogs, passing aircraft and young Visigoths roaring around on motorcycles.

First, we transmitted a sequence of notes, harmonies and chords, using a synthesiser and our own voices. The sounds around us immediately faded, the cloudbank above us dispersed and the sky became blue.

Then we did a brief visualisation exercise, to seal the energy the planet had received, and the public had generated, in the two weeks before and after Diana's funeral. I volunteered to be the 'anchor', and let the others do the visualisation.

This is what they saw:

Amanda
The colour red came to me – a brilliant red, which turned into fire and flames. Every time I took a breath, the flames rose higher and

grew more intense; then the dragon's wings came out of the fire, and its scales were earth-coloured.

I was sitting on the dragon's back, and with the last note I sang it took off vertically into the sky and I went with it. When I opened my eyes, you were all enveloped in a silvery, purple/blue haze.

Tim

I saw bright red, and what seemed to be a face in the redness, and two enormous eyes which opened as I watched. I saw the outline of a five-pointed star kaleidoscoping in the brilliance of the colour. When I opened my eyes, the sun was a bright silver and there was a blue haze over everybody.

I had pictured a golden, sleeping dragon before the vision began, and during the vision it woke.

Bran

I was standing away from the planet at the level of the moon, watching a dragon to the right-hand side of the Earth throwing a huge, crystalline net round the globe, in the manner of a Chinese fisherman. The dragon had glints of red and purple in his skin; I think he was a Chinese dragon, and he was standing on his tail, using his front legs to cast the net. He knew exactly what he was doing.

I now feel quite certain that the Earth is safe . . .

Peter

First I saw pink — a mixture of brilliant red and silvery white, and within it a device like the three feet of the Isle of Man symbol, which began to revolve. I then saw that this symbol was on the forehead of my rainbow dragon, like a third eye.

"It swirled faster and faster, becoming an enormous crystalline globe, encircling the Earth herself, and I knew that, although there is still further work to be done to 'wake the dragons' around the planet, this particular operation is now complete: the matrix is in position and ready to do its job.

No wonder she had – and still has – so many fans around the world: Diana was the living embodiment of 'the walking wounded' – which means just about all of us. How many people do you know who *don't* carry the scars of mental and emotional damage done to them at school, at home or out in the world?

e-mail from a friend in California
October, 1997

I once wrote that Diana, Princess of Wales was the most loved person in the world. Now that she has been taken from us, I realise that my words were not strong enough. Diana was a treasure; not just a national treasure, for her light was too bright to shine in one country alone, but a treasure to be shared with the world. The unprecedented level of worldwide grief for her has shown that the people's princess had no equal and can never be replaced.

Michael O'Mara

7

Reflections on the Goddess as Princess of Hearts

e-mailed September, 1997 by Sharon Whiteman in Australia
to Krystyna Spicer in California to Jan Goldstoff of the
Women of Vision, New York

Yve Betar

WHEN DIANA, Princess of Wales was officially declared dead in Paris, I had to sit down, cry and let myself feel the loss of this remarkable woman. I remembered when I'd seen what was probably her most famous interview, about two years ago, in which she spoke of the need to think with our hearts, not just our heads; of trying to define a new role for herself as an ambassador; of being unwilling to buckle under to the rigid dictates of the Monarchy, and of hoping to become a Queen of people's hearts rather than of Great Britain. It had hit me then: the mythic proportion of her life, and what a huge 'contract' or mission she must have taken on for her short visit to planet Earth.

I realised then — and still believe — that she is one of the women who have been working to bring the 'Essential Feminine' or Goddess energy into the planet in a new, more balanced, more vulnerable, poignant and relevant way. I am not saying that she was necessarily aware of this consciously. Nevertheless, it was what she did.

And as someone who cares about the conscious evolution of the planet and the return of the Goddess in all Her forms and aspects, I feel an immense sense of gratitude.

When she stepped into her larger-than-life role at the age of nineteen, Diana became the modern day symbol of Cinderella, the beautiful, sweet and kind but unknown young woman from a broken home, who was destined – in our minds, as believers in the fairy tale – to get married and live 'happily ever after'.

Cinderella was a convenient ideal of an archaic patriarchal system, whose life was defined by, and built solely around, her husband and his position in society. Her story was complete, and considered to have had a happy ending, once she was married to Prince Charming. Whatever went on in her life after that was no longer relevant, as far as the fairy tale was concerned.

It was Diana's job to shake our heads loose and help us to realise that a myth embodying such a superficial and restricted view of the value and meaning of women's lives, needs and potential would no longer do.

What moved me most about Diana's life was that she reinforced in me the belief that it is the process of life itself that is important. Few public figures have ever shared their process so vulnerably. When Cinderella confessed to bulimia, the world could no longer see eating disorders and the media-inspired beliefs and images that underlie them as unimportant or harmless.

Diana reinforced the growing awareness that denial – trying to hide the shameful bits of our lives, lying in order to try and project an acceptable image – was no longer an appropriate solution to the problems we all face and the choices we make when dealing with them.

A Course in Miracles claims that our safety lies not in attack or defence but in our defencelessness – in our vulnerability. The internal voices that try to convince us that our shame is real would have us believe that truth and openness will lead to condemnation.

But the Princess demonstrated otherwise.

Three other important issues stand out to me as aspects of what will become part of Diana's mythic legacy:

Much has been said of her good works, of the break-throughs in perception that she helped to initiate about AIDS, leprosy, starving children, land mines and other humanitarian issues. She was truly a channel of Heart energy and helped to bring in, expand and ground humanitarian values. As a mother and through her charity work, she lived out the 'Good Mother'/Mother Mary/Mother Teresa/Demeter part of the Feminine archetype.

But to me, her real gift was that she also brought in a greater sense of internal balance. She was not a flat, one-sided channel for Goddess energy.

Aphrodite, the alchemical Goddess of sensuality, sexuality, creativity, passion and life force energy was also alive in her – as well as a myriad other Divine Feminine energies.

The Venus/Aphrodite archetype has really only recently re-emerged from the shadows. Marilyn Monroe and then Madonna have become icons who symbolised two different stages of her re-emergence into the culture. In these two women, Aphrodite could be seen as mirroring the obverse side of the Mother Mary archetype. Marilyn represented a young, naïve, abused Aphrodite emerging after thousands of years of denial, suppression and abuse.

Madonna was bolder and more rebellious, flagrantly defying accepted definitions of the 'old feminine' and reminding each of us of the work we need to do to recognise, embrace and heal our internal shadow aspects so that we can reclaim their power and life force energy as part of our own wholeness. In Diana, we move on to a more reclaimed and integrated Aphrodite energy. Diana was a sexy, alive, vibrant woman who could get down and boogie as well as do good works.

In a way we could say that she symbolised the beginning of the end of the outdated 'madonna/prostitute' (good girl/bad girl) either/or dichotomy that has been, for so long, a part of our cultural view of women.

I pray that this marks the beginning of a time when young girls will be taught to value and cherish the vibrancy, sensuality and sexuality that is part of their Aphrodite aspect and that never again will they be called 'tramps' or 'sluts' by those who feel threatened by this energy.

Diana's life and death also brought boundary and privacy issues strongly into public awareness. I find this especially significant as I have been processing boundary issues in my own life for the past five years or so, but in quite a different way. It is also somewhat poignant and ironic because the Goddess Diana/Artemis was the archetype that represented the ability to set clearly-defined boundaries and to say 'no' when she meant 'no'. When a hunter was caught watching the Goddess and her nymphs at her Sacred Pool, she turned him into a stag. When the stag ran away, he was shot by his own former hunting companions.

Our Diana had no such powers in life, but perhaps in death she will help us to see that everyone, even a Goddess/Princess, needs boundaries that are inviolate and must be respected when she – or we ourselves – say 'no'.

Diana also represents an evolutionary leap for the Goddess Hera, 'Queen of Heaven', who was devalued by the patriarchy and betrayed by her husband Zeus. During the 'dark night' episode of Hera's story that comes down to us in mythology, her 'shadow' side emerged and she took revenge on the other women. Chroniclers saw her as a shrew.

Through Princess Diana, Hera fared somewhat better, emerging as a woman of dignity as well as vulnerability and living up to her role as Queen, if not of Heaven or Great Britain, then certainly of people's hearts.

When a person lives out part of the evolution of an archetypal or mythic story with global implications, then their story must be witnessed for its complete value to be received. My intention today is to bear witness Princess Diana's key role in a deep, archetypal, mythic process of evolution.

I see our Princess as quite publicly sharing her process of reclaiming her power and authenticity by rising like a phoenix from the ashes of a dying, co-dependent, disempowering Cinderella fantasy.

As a woman, she modelled dealing with problems and issues rather than hiding from them, denying them or putting on a false front. I see her as an inspiration especially to women who want to take the risk of being authentically themselves rather than a composite of what they think everyone else wants them to be.

She was a person who faced many challenges, who had lots of learning experiences (i.e. made lots of mistakes) and kept coming back stronger, healthier, more mature and more 'heart present'. I do see her as a Queen of Hearts and sometimes even as an Avatar, a Bodhisattva or a goddess. To some this may sound extreme, but what she did, she did not only for herself, but for each of us. Did Jesus or Buddha know at the time that the process in which they were participating was bigger than life and would benefit all of us? I doubt it.

If she had not died so tragically and mythically, I can imagine her giving a speech on her 100th birthday, reminding women that the most important thing to remember is to be true to themselves; and that we *don't* have to match some media image of perfection to be perfectly, uniquely and wonderfully ourselves.

Or perhaps she is whispering this very message right now — from a dimension beyond the range of normal hearing, on a wavelength that can only be received by our hearts.

Namaste, Princess Diana.

We honour the Goddess within you.

8

The Lake
and the Sword

From the rose of the shires
comes the most beautiful rose of all: you, Diana.
I believe you were only loaned to us by God
to show us our weaknesses.

Alan Masters

Kingsland Avenue, Kingsthorpe
Letter pinned to the gates of Althorp Park, Northampton

A FEW DOZEN well-wishers were waiting patiently outside the curved, wrought iron gates of Althorp Park, despite a sign announcing that the house was closed. A number of small bouquets and cards lay on the ground, and several more formal flower arrangements lay on the grass at the edge of the private park.

I told the duty officer I had brought a personal message for Lord Spencer from a member of Diana's family. The man telephoned the house, and a few minutes later a car approached.

The driver, a young security guard, climbed out and opened the gates. I gave him the envelope. He took it back to the car and drove off to the house.

7 p.m. Suddenly exhausted after a night without sleep, I sat back in my seat and closed my eyes as the London-bound train gathered

speed. At that moment a small voice in my head said, "Take a look out of the window."

I pried my eyes open and did so. And what I saw literally brought me to my feet, all tiredness forgotten:

The sun had just set, and to the south the entire sky was awash with apricot/pink and gold. In this sky, stretching away to infinity, was an inner landscape of mountains, plains and gently-sloping hills.

Above it were two gigantic upraised wings, like those of an Archangel. And in the foreground . . . a lake bordered by trees, its still surface broken only by the tip of a gigantic, golden sword-blade, at least fifteen miles long!

The hilt of the sword, high in the sky to my left, was also gold, and fully three miles wide.

And where the tip of the blade pierced the surface of the lake was a small, brilliant oblong of dazzling gold.

This astonishing tableau didn't slowly drift and fade, the way skyscapes invariably do: it held its shape *for more than twenty minutes*. The other two passengers in the carriage kept looking out of their windows to see what I was so engrossed in – but they appeared to see nothing out of the ordinary: they both resumed reading their newspapers.

Eventually, the outskirts of London obscured the view, and I sat down. *Now* I had something to report to Andrew!

This was the ultimate confirmation of everything that had been happening in the last three weeks, to all of us. It was the full choir and orchestra, proclaiming:

The Sword is now in safe hands. The Succession to the British Throne is now in safe hands.

And even more than these:

The vast outpouring of light, love and power that encircled the globe when Diana left us has now been earthed, and stored, and is now available to everyone, whenever and wherever we feel the need to call on it. In other words, we are *all* in safe hands now.

9

The Diana phenomenon

An insight into the meaning of the Princess's death
Peter Dawkins

THE PHENOMENON OF GRIEF and the outpouring of love which followed Diana's death was unprecedented in recorded history, with billions of people involved worldwide.

Why?

Diana was not a saint in the accepted view, but she was certainly seen to be a good and compassionate person. It was her very humanity and her ability to communicate with, and both physically and emotionally 'touch' the other person, particularly the deprived or injured, which moved people's hearts. Moreover she was *seen* to do this, and she did so despite the requirements of etiquette and regardless of personal safety. She was also seen and known to be an injured person herself, with human weaknesses which she did not and could not hide – although she might have tried to hide them at the beginning.

Diana's unique circumstances made these matters and herself very public – far more public than any other person in world history. Indeed the very things that gave her the publicity and fame which made 'the Diana phenomenon' possible were the same things that injured much of her personal life and pushed her to her death.

An arranged marriage to 'the world's most eligible bachelor'; her subsequent demanding role as Princess of Wales and potential Queen of Great Britain; mother of a future King of Great Britain; the glamour attached to all this, combined with her own personal glamour and attractiveness; and the intense interest of the media and their exploitation of her as a figurehead and role model which made her into a star – while at the same time they tried to destroy her and her husband's image by finding or inventing every fault possible.

Even though only a princess, Diana was *made* a queen. She could not avoid this, and ultimately it led to her own desire to be the "queen of people's hearts".

In this she succeeded far more than anyone realised, until her death revealed it. But during her life, her own heart was laid open and attacked. She could not protect it, nor could anyone else; or, if they could, they chose not to. And so she died – her heart died, the Queen of people's hearts died, and perhaps therefore something in people's own hearts died.

Perhaps this is what we were really grieving.

Because our response to Diana's death was far wider and greater and deeper than reason and experience dictate for the death of one person, however famous.

What, therefore, *was* Diana? (As distinct from, "*Who* was Diana?")

She was playing a role on the world stage – a role which she herself finally recognised and proclaimed – the Queen of Hearts. This is an ancient, archetypal role. It is also a role especially related to Great Britain – the role of Britannia herself, queen of the spiritual heart chakra of the world, sometimes called the chakra of the Holy Spirit.

Like Queen Elizabeth I before her, Diana personified the celestial Queen – the Grail Queen. Without fully realising it, the media built up this image and gave it out to the world. Even Diana's name was appropriate for her role, for Diana is one of the titles of the celestial Queen, who is also known as Mary the mother, and as Europa or Persephone the beautiful, and as Hermione, the harmony of the heart.

Twin sister of Apollo, the sun god, Diana is the moon goddess – the intelligence that reflects and makes manifest the wisdom of the heart.

As chaste Diana the huntress, she was herself hunted by those who misunderstood the true meaning of virginity. As Diana/Artemis she was and remains the protector of all children and of all those who are pure in heart – but hunter and destroyer of the impure and those who would harm the innocents.

Princess Diana certainly fulfilled something of this role, especially with her campaign for the worldwide abolition of land mines.

In the sky, the goddess Diana is represented both by the Pleiades and Ursa Minor, wherein we find the North Pole star – which marks the possible entry of the world into a Golden Age.

Diana is also celebrated as Cassiopeia, the celestial Queen, whose stars are her children of light. There is a tradition that, whenever a new star is born in this constellation, or a great light shines out from one of her existing stars, it marks the birth of a great light on Earth, a Christ manifestation. The central star of Cassiopeia was seen to blaze spectacularly the day before Princess Diana's car accident.

Every death is a birth at another level. The death of a great person can raise the level of consciousness and life of many others. What is called the birth of a star in Cassiopeia is usually the death of a pre-existing star, such as the supernova of 1572–74 which announced the birth of the Baconian/Rosicrucian light on Earth.

But each starburst which destroys a star sends the star's light and substance out across the Universe as a gift to other worlds, seeding them with new light and increasing their own inherent glory. The ancient Mayans – the 'mother race' of America – left a record of our own times, which forecast that the 25-year period corresponding to our years 1987–2012 is of major significance to the planet and mankind. During this period there is a coming together of two cycles, or 'Universes', which creates a gateway in time through which we may leap from our own Universe into another, higher one.

This solar gateway has a series of steps and doors in it. It opened on the day of the Harmonic Convergence in 1987 when, for the first time, millions of people around the world joined together in prayer and meditation on this theme. Other such days of intense spiritual focus have been taking place ever since, at pre-arranged times. But on the day of Princess Diana's death and throughout the week following, there took place something else – something belonging to this great gateway, something related to the harmony that is gradually manifesting in the world – yet even more than this:

The interpreters of the Mayan Calendar refer to this date as "stepping into Sun consciousness". There are, I have been informed, three such stages or steps, all of which are due to take place before the end of this century or Millennium.

The day of Diana's death was the day we took our first step into planetary Sun consciousness.

A few months after Diana's funeral, I sent the following gift for Prince William and Prince Harry to Earl Spencer, who was kind enough to reply:

> *"I very much like the text of your gift for William and Harry. I do not believe they are ready for it though, so I will hang onto it on their behalf, and give it to them at some later stage. I hope that you approve of that decision?"*

Several years have elapsed since then, so I feel sure that Lord Spencer will have given it to his nephews by now . . .

10

A personal
A to Z

A gift for Prince William and Prince Harry
as they set out into a new century,
a new Millennium and a new world.

MUCH HAS BEEN SAID about your mother's concern that your Royal duties and obligations should not be allowed to deprive you of a sense of fun and enjoyment; that you should be free to balance formal occasions with more relaxed ones; and that your private life should be respected.

Achieving this should present no problem. Those around you are surely too experienced to make the mistake of underestimating Diana's influence and example; there are signs that they are beginning, however reluctantly, to recognise the immensity of her achievement – an achievement that no-one could possibly have foreseen – and have experienced for themselves the global admiration and affection that she commands, even now.

You are about to embark, not just on one great adventure, but two: preparing for public life as heirs to the Throne, and stepping out with us all into the uncharted territory of a new century and a new Millennium.

To help you on your way, please accept this personal guidebook, which has been designed to make your journey as enjoyable and fulfilling as possible. Never forget, wherever you go you will have the support and encouragement of all those millions of 'ordinary' folk (*she* knew they were anything but ordinary) who were united in their love and affection for Diana, and in their respect for the superb instinct and intuition that guided her throughout her public life.

the Battle for the Earth

All too clearly, the Battle for the Earth is already being waged – within us and around us. Perhaps 'battle for the soul of mankind' would be a more accurate way of expressing it: exhausted by centuries of needless conflict, hatred, oppression and war, the human race is now beginning to reach out for some other, less painful way of conducting its affairs.

As a result, we are now faced with a major decision. And there is no other way of putting this: the choice we make will decide the fate of the world. It is World Referendum time, no less, and as the milestone year 2000 hurtles past us, we are being asked to choose, and to work for, one of the two following Parties:

the Dark	the Light
hatred	love
vengeance	forgiveness
callousness	compassion
cruelty	kindness
greed	generosity
selfishness	selflessness
hoarding	sharing
profiteering	giving value
oppression	tolerance

slavery	freedom
hostility	friendship
war	peace
death	life

a beginning

One of the unsigned cards attached to the railings outside Buckingham Palace in September, 1997 said,

"A light has gone out across the world." And although it certainly felt that way, the reverse is also true: When Diana left us, a great light encircled the planet, dissolving frontiers of race, creed and colour, revealing the ideals that so many of us share, and – who knows? – maybe even heralding the world that most of us are yearning for.

The most effective way to protect Diana's legacy will be to follow her example in our everyday lives. If we succeed in doing so, her abrupt departure will no longer be seen as the end of anything, but as the beginning of something truly momentous for us all.

Britain

Britain once played a major role on the world stage; she enjoyed enormous power, influence and prestige; her Empire straddled the globe. There was much to be admired in this great enterprise, and – it has to be said – much to be deplored. The motives and methods of those who built that Empire were sometimes honourable and far-sighted, at other times ruthless and inhumane.

Britain still has a vital role to play in the world – as an example of hard-won wisdom, courage, compassion and justice. But she can only play that role if we are *all* prepared to embody that wisdom, that courage, that compassion and that justice.

And to achieve this, we must haul ourselves out of the swamp of greedy, soulless, selfish materialism that engulfed the world during the 1980s . . .

character

Our personality is our 'front', but our character is our *real* self:

> our loyalty
> our honesty
> our independence of mind
> our courage
> our generosity
> our determination
> our sympathy
> our capacity for friendship
> our tolerance
> . . . *or their opposites!*

courage

It takes courage to say, "No thanks" when we're tempted by those around us to indulge in things we know are no good for us. Anyone can run with the herd, but it takes character and inner strength to say no — and *not* to feel superior for having done so.

It also takes courage to recognise that we might not know it all, and that other people might have something to teach us. In recent years there have been encouraging signs that men are beginning to entertain the possibility that they might have something to learn from women . . .

death

Throughout the last century, evidence to suggest that physical death might not be the end of the story continued to mount. It is now believed by a huge and ever-increasing number of people – including the many who have reported that, during a near-death experience, they briefly found themselves in another world or dimension altogether – that when our lives here are over, we continue our journey on another level, and that when we arrive there, we are reunited with everyone we have loved and thought we had lost.

It has also been reported that, in these 'higher' worlds – which we sometimes visit while we sleep – time isn't chopped up into weeks, days, hours, minutes and seconds, as it is here: it is more of a natural, continuous flow. And, by all accounts, these worlds are themselves not yet perfect – they too are gradually moving *towards* perfection . . .

the deep end

Some people tend to spend most of their time in the shallow end, and neither experience nor achieve much during their lives. Others are thrown in at the deep end, early on – and if they manage to stay afloat, they learn rather more than those at the other end of the pool.

You were thrown in at the deep end, and you have both dealt commendably with everything that has been thrown at you. (Your strength comes from your father's *and* your mother's lines.)

In time, you will probably be grateful for most of these ordeals and initiations, although some of them have been extremely painful.

Remember, our pain is the fire in which our character is forged. Fine steel owes its mettle to the heat of the furnace!

Diana

Your mother left us in an unparalleled blaze of glory. (No-one's death has ever been mourned by so many people around the world.) That blaze of glory is the flame that we must take great care to shield and protect, as it can light our path into the new Millennium. May we never lose sight of her priceless legacy, her crowning achievement, her parting gift to us all:

The weeks that shook the world in the autumn of 1997 are proof positive that the power of compassion and unconditional love surpasses all other human enterprises: if we get our love and forgiveness right, *every wrong on Earth begins to right itself.*

With respect, neither politics nor good intentions alone can pull off 'the Big One': only love with its sleeves rolled up will do it. Diana and her mentor, Mother Teresa, had their sleeves rolled up. So how about we all get off our duffs and follow suit?

It doesn't have to be grim, hard work — it might even be fun. We can *make* it so . . .

Empires

Today's Empires are industrial, commercial and technological, rather than territorial. They would do well to learn from history: serve the people, and you will thrive and grow; exploit the people, and eventually you will collapse . . .

Excalibur

Excalibur was, and is, the Sword of Truth and Justice. It is best wielded by someone who knows how to use it, when to use it, and why. It was last unsheathed by Earl Spencer in Westminster Abbey on Saturday, 6 September 1997. Half a lifetime ago, it was taken up on our behalf by his kinsman, Winston Churchill. It is now in safe hands, awaiting the time when it will next be called upon . . .

forgiveness

Forgiveness is one of love's most powerful relations. It can heal wounds just as quickly as unconditional love. In a sense, it *is* unconditional love . . .

friends

Kings, Princes, the rich, the powerful and the beautiful share a common problem: "How do we know who our real friends are — and who are pretending to be friends to serve their own ends?"

One answer might be, "By using our intuition. By honing and sharpening the instinct that enables us to discriminate between the genuine and the false."

This intuition is possibly the greatest ally you will ever have: it will tell you which members of your circle are being honest and open, and which have hidden agendas of their own . . .

the future

The future depends on every single one of us. We can no longer afford to sit back and let 'them' create it for us — whoever 'they' might be. The time has come for us to build it *ourselves* . . .

kingship

A wise king is someone who knows his people, understands their needs, feels for them in their struggles, shares their grief and their joy, delights in their achievements, is tolerant of their failings; likes them, condemns no-one, and does what he can to uphold their morale and lift their spirit.

A wise king stands back from the hurly-burly, declines to take sides, is no slave of fashion, bestows favour only when it is truly deserved, and calmly watches the pageant unfold before him.

He is a friend to his people, a brother and, in later years, a father. His instinct tells him when to be intimate with them, and when to step back a little. That way, the Crown is both strengthened and protected.

Above all, a King can remind us of our own potential greatness. In all this he is the servant, not the master, of his people. In his humility lies his strength . . .

love

How many kinds of love can there be? There is the love we have for life itself; for our world, who supplies all our needs and endures all our assaults on her without complaining; for our country; for our parents and our family; for certain older folk who were kind to us; for our friends; for children; for animals and birds; for a place, for a particular house or home; for times long gone but not forgotten; for music, for films, for certain kinds of food; for our hobbies, pastimes and sports.

And what of the love we feel for our lover? Is it unconditional – or is it a kind of emotional power game, a balancing act? Does it make us feel good? Does it increase our confidence and well-being?

Does it inspire us? Is it more desire than love? Is it more need than love? Does it give more pain than joy? Is it addictive? Are we nothing without it – or are we whole in spite of it?

Love is one of those mysteries we need an entire lifetime – or several lifetimes – to explore . . .

mistakes

We can probably learn more from our own – and other people's – mistakes and failures than we can from our successes. Most of our lives are a struggle between negative and positive, within us and around us. It pays to recognise, to acknowledge and to control our own negativity, and to understand other people's – without judging or condemning ourselves and each other . . .

opposition

As we live in a world of duality – right/wrong, weak/strong, generous/mean, kind/cruel, rich/poor, etc. – anyone who chooses justice, freedom, peace and equality tends to attract opposition from those whose affluence and power depend on injustice, oppression, war and inequality – and who will not hesitate to fight if they feel that their position is being threatened.

We can learn as much from our opponents as we can from our friends . . .

pain

A few years ago Merlin said:

> *"We have all known pain, and somehow survived it. We have all caused pain, and come to regret it. By absorbing some of the pain of this world and that of our fellow man – and by giving it back, not as anger, violence and a desire for revenge, but as hard-won wisdom and love and experience – we become alchemists, true magicians; no longer part of the problem, but of the solution."*

He might very well have been referring to Diana herself.

the past is past

Maybe some terrible things were done to us or to our people, long ago. We should let it lie — *we* don't have to get even: life itself has a way of settling old scores, however long it might take.

Anyway, emotional luggage is too darned heavy to carry around with us wherever we go . . .

politics

The word 'politics' comes from the Greek word *polites*, meaning 'citizen'. Politicians and citizens alike, please note . . .

revenge

The desire for revenge is a malignant cancer that eats away at the avenger, and *not* at the target of his vengeance . . .

sharing

We have always been encouraged to get whatever we can, even at the expense of everyone around us. This makes us all permanent competitors, enemies. Nothing less than a 180° turnaround in our thinking is now called for: if we decide to start *sharing* what is available, suddenly we all become allies — and the desperate struggle for survival becomes a rapidly receding nightmare of the past . . .

strength

Most of us are strong in one way or another – physically, mentally, emotionally or spiritually. The most rewarding way to use that strength is to share it with others who might need some of it; to use our strength *against* each other is to destroy part of the fabric of our lives . . .

the Throne

One of the highest accomplishments of a King or a Prince is his natural ability to share *himself* with the people and, by doing so, to dispense some of the light and power that emanate from the Throne.

Diana had this ability to a remarkable degree, which is one of the reasons why she found a place for herself in so many people's hearts . . .

tolerance

Why do we look down on people of different social standing, colour or culture from ourselves? Why do we ridicule them for their purported lack of taste or intelligence or breeding? By doing so, we reveal ourselves as deluded, snobbish, inadequate.

How sad that our own confidence and self-assurance are so often based on our contempt for others, rather than on our own strength of character.

All paths lead, eventually, to the truth, to perfection, to what many people think of as God. Which means that your path, or our path, or their path isn't *better* than any other, but simply different . . .

tradition

At its best, tradition passes on from generation to generation the finest that a nation or a people has to offer. The tradition of honour, integrity and service can only be admired.

But there are other traditions too, some of them centuries old — of cruelty, vengeance, hatred and oppression. And the inheritors of those traditions have always been prepared to defend them at any cost . . .

when it's our time to go

What will they say when we go on our way? Will we leave the world a better place for our having been here? Will they be glad or sorry to see us go?

Or will our lives make no difference to anyone, either way?

Only we can answer those questions. By doing the best we can. By holding fast to what we perceive to be right and true.

And by being the best we can be . . .

whole people

Throughout history, the nations have largely been run by men, and women have been obliged to devote most of their time and energy to creating and nurturing children and making life comfortable for their menfolk. Although this system has worked, it is not without serious flaws:

Man — the hunter/killer, warrior, trail-blazer and Empire-builder — has been so intent on carving out his place in society that he has tended to regard such things as intuition, compassion, gentleness and emotion as exclusively the province of women.

And woman — the mother, teacher, nurse, home-maker — has

been so preoccupied by these important duties that she has neglected her own intellect and creativity and tended to leave the thinking, planning and doing to her menfolk.

Result? We have run the risk of ending up with a race of largely insensitive men and passive women. There is a lot of evidence to suggest that most of the problems facing us today result from this serious imbalance. And there are also encouraging signs that thinking men and women are now alert to this danger and taking steps to avert it.

It has become clear that men would do well to 'borrow' from women some of that intuition, compassion, gentleness and emotion – which men also possess, needless to say, but have tended to suppress; and women would do well to 'borrow' from men some of their get-up-and-go, decisiveness and powers of organisation. A growing number of men and women are already doing so, of course.

In other words, much will be achieved when men and women declare a truce, join forces as equal creative partners and start to rebuild human society *together*, from the ground up. In this manner, we can all become whole.

In future, young people will be encouraged from the earliest age to take an interest in their own *and each other's* growth and development. Helping each other will, at the very least, become as important as competing with each other . . .

world citizens

Every nation has its own particular genius, and has added something unique to the world. There is no reason at all why we shouldn't be proud of our country. But there are many powerful reasons why we who live in these islands should now begin to think of ourselves not just as British, or even European, but as world citizens. Which is not easy for a people who, for centuries, have anxiously scanned the horizon for approaching longboats, galleons, submarines, aircraft and rockets!

Like it or not – and despite a long and bloody history of hostility and war – we, the peoples of the world *need* each other. Take Britons, for example: other countries supply much of our food, resources and raw materials. Our very survival depends on the goodwill of these nations, and on their need for what we, in turn, have to offer them.

Her extraordinary life and career conspired to turn a very private, very English girl, Diana Spencer, into a world citizen – possibly the most famous there has ever been and ever will be.

She worked her magic wherever she went, here and overseas; her natural generosity of spirit made her reach out to *anyone* in distress, irrespective of their race, creed, colour or background.

As a result, long before she left us, Diana no longer belonged to the British Isles alone, but to the world. We might not quite be able to achieve what she did, in so spectacular a fashion, but we would do well to follow her example.

How? By beginning to think about what we all have in common, what we all need, what we all have to *give*, rather than what we can *get* from each other.

Diana was fearless: she got out there and proved that kindness and loving concern, which cost nothing other than a little time and a little effort, can sweep aside every barrier, obstacle, frontier and dividing wall in existence. *This* was her greatest gift to us all: a priceless legacy we would be crazy to dismiss or ignore.

11

The Fifth Energy

*The four constituent energies, or 'building
blocks', of the physical Universe are said to be
electromagnetism, gravity, strong atomic force, and weak
atomic force.*

DURING THE PAST thirty years, thanks largely to Merlin, my
friends and I had begun to learn something of the four
'Guardians', or universal energies:

> **the Lady** (the divine Mother – love/wisdom);
> her consort, **the Magician** (the heavenly Father
> – creative intelligence);
> **the King** (will, order);
> and **the Master of Ceremonies**, (the mystic,
> sometimes known as 'the lord of misrule' or
> the joker in the pack).

Then in the autumn of 1996, Merlin asked Peter Quiller to visit
Britain's major power sites, in order to carry out some major
realignment and activation work.

While exploring the Lammermuir Hills in Scotland, Peter was
amazed and excited to detect the presence of a fifth energy. A while
later he came to see me in London, and asked if I could intuit what
it might be.

The moment he asked, I felt as if a cloak had been placed round my shoulders — or rather, as if I was wearing a one-piece suit of silver-grey body armour, made not of chain-mail but of some unknown substance, as soft as a bird's feathers yet as strong as steel. It seemed to be offering me the challenge to go beyond what I thought I was — to assume a slightly different, more advanced role.

"I can only describe it as a unique combination of feminine and masculine energies, working together in perfect harmony," I said.

Peter nodded. "That's exactly what I got! A powerful synthesis of the energies."

A thought came to me: "Before man and woman made their first appearance, it's said that we were *all* androgynous. Which the angels still are," I added as an afterthought.

Ever since that day, I have thought of this 'new' energy as 'the Androgyne'.

A year or so later, I decided to ask Merlin to throw a little more light on the matter. Here is part of our conversation:

MJ

What is the Androgyne?

Merlin

It has no gender, and will probably be sensed by men as a feminine presence, and by women as a masculine one. An *inner* presence, not an outer one. Or, if you prefer, the bridge between the two!

MJ

What is its relationship to the four Guardian energies?

Merlin

It is the key component with which Nature works; the basic building-block out of which this particular Universe was constructed. It is a bi-polar, subatomic particle, the very foundation stone of physical Creation, of duality itself! Moreover, it is *amenable to thought*. Hence the saying, "Mind over matter."

> Which leads us to the intriguing proposition that you *are* your thoughts, and you merely hire your bodies from the wardrobe department!

MJ

How will we recognise the Androgyne's presence?

Merlin

It will vary with each person. Some will welcome it, others will resist its subtle influence. *You* have been aware of it all your life – without knowing what it was.

MJ

What is the function or purpose of the Androgyne?

Merlin

The Earth herself, and all of you who wish to 'come along for the ride', are about to rise into a new dimension. The Androgyne has come to help you make this transition.

MJ

Why now?

Merlin

Why *not* now?! It is high time the human race emerged from the cocoon and reclaimed its full stature and magnificence.

MJ

Will everyone sense the presence of the new energy?

Merlin

Almost certainly not. No-one who is comfortably entrenched in long-established systems will see any need for anything 'new'. This is not *new*, of course, but part of your original constitution, your wholeness, which for untold ages you have been reluctant to acknowledge or recognise.

MJ

Forgive the repetition, but why now?

Merlin

Throughout recorded history, human society has been governed by men: the counsel of women has been largely disregarded. The resulting imbalance has manifested as perpetual conflict, aggression, expansion, terrorism, war, espionage, mistrust, paranoia and fear.

[*a sardonic smile*]

Not the healthiest foundations upon which to build a civilisation, it could be said!

If they are to build a new kind of human society, a new civilisation on Earth, men will not only have to seek the counsel of women, they will have to acknowledge that part of their *own* nature that is 'feminine'.

MJ

And in order for women to become equal partners with men during these all-important rebuilding operations, they must begin to acknowledge those elements within them that could be described as 'masculine'?

Merlin

Precisely.

MJ

But life is pretty hard going, so men have always *had* to act tough, and can hardly be blamed for always having looked on gentleness – in themselves, at least – as a sign of weakness.

Merlin

It has been said many times before, but it bears repeating: only by maintaining a perfect balance between male and female energies will you attain your full potential, and equip yourselves for the onward journey.

He glowers at me, and from his throat comes a sound like the growl of a bear.

Whatever your warlords might believe, this galaxy is *not* going to be taken like an enemy blockhouse on Pork Chop hill. Others have tried – and come to grief. The Universe must be approached with humility and a willingness to learn – it will *not* surrender its secrets to combat soldiers bristling with military hardware!

MJ

So where does all this leave us? Is it too late to restore the balance?

Merlin

No – but you must start *now*. On the largest possible scale. Conventional politics and economics will have to defer to the urgent matter that now confronts you: the business of lifting yourselves and your planet out of the mire.

Make no mistake: an extraordinary destiny awaits you – but you will *never* reach those heights until you acknowledge and then dispense with your primal fears, your aggression and hostility. After many gruelling years as undergraduates in the physical University, you are being invited to graduate!

It is no accident that the Androgyne has chosen this particular moment to re-enter the arena. It knows you can't do it unassisted.

MJ

But so many people are terrified of change — especially if it means having to give up deeply-engrained habits and customs.

The Magician nods, then sits forward in his chair, to emphasise his next point.

Merlin

Remember, the process involves *no* surrender.

On the contrary: by acknowledging their 'feminine' qualities, men will *not* become lesser men, weaker men, but will be all the stronger for it! And women will welcome it!

And by acknowledging their own 'masculine' attributes, women themselves will not become any less feminine — they will simply shed some of the characteristics that have *never* served them well, such as helplessness, passivity and an exaggerated dependency on the male of the species — which men, it must be said, have done little to discourage! This process will gradually bring to an end the age-old conflict that has long undermined the man/woman relationship.

MJ

Was Diana, Princess of Wales, an example of the fifth energy?

Merlin

Heavens be praised — I wondered if you'd ask that!

I hoped you'd ask that. Of course she was. She conspicuously embodied both sides of the coin: her beauty, compassion and sensuality were essentially feminine; and her independence, self-determination and daring, essentially masculine.

MJ

Predictably, the latter got her into a lot of hot water with the old guard — diehards and traditionalists who expected her to endure all the humiliations and betrayals, and not to strike back.

Merlin

[*a nod*]

The last gasp of the outgoing patriarchal order.

He fixes me with a piercing, professorial gaze.

To sum up: the arrival of the fifth energy implies no surrender, no loss. It heralds your imminent completion – a gigantic step forward in your journey.

[*a brief smile*]

The Androgyne offers you a pass-key to your ascended selves – and a foretaste of the divinity you seem to have forgotten or mislaid, and must now retrieve.

We later found out that the Androgyne, or fifth energy, had been 'discovered' in Italy in 1938, but the physicist concerned was ridiculed, and his theories regarding its nature and function discredited by the scientific establishment of his day.

Merlin's words kept coming back to me:

> *"This is no new archetype, of course, but part of your original constitution, your wholeness, which for untold ages you have refused to acknowledge or recognise."*

Which set me thinking: 1400 years ago, what was one of the first duties of the Grail knight? To 'rescue damsels in distress'. This could have had *two* meanings, one outer, the other inner:

It could have meant giving women the respect that is their due, treating them as – at the very least – equals; *and* to rescue 'the damsel locked in the tower' – which was surely the warrior/ knight's own gentler nature, buried deep inside him!

Had Merlin and Arthur's mission not been sabotaged, who knows how many centuries of agony Europe and the wider world might have been spared?

By persistently ignoring these universal truths, and ruthlessly pursuing our personal, material and territorial aims, we have brought the world and ourselves to the brink of ruin. Maybe now, at long, long last we shall pause, and think and act accordingly . . .

Scientists find 'God's particle'

Headline in The Sunday Times
London, 10 September, 2000

The British physicist who has just 'discovered' this particle will probably win the Nobel Prize for having done so!

Merlin and Peter Quiller, take a bow . . .

The colossal wave of love she triggered when she left us might possibly have been the equivalent of the energy she was *meant* to have released, had her life not been cut short. Who knows?

One thing is certain: to identify her merely as 'an English rose' is to do her much less than justice: as the two billion people who are still grieving for her instinctively understand, she represents something far greater than that — with all respect to English roses which, as you know, I used to cultivate in my garden in Wiltshire!

Simon Peter Fuller
December, 1997

12

Damage limitation (i)

When you lose someone you love,
you gain an angel you know.

Oprah Winfrey

IN APRIL 1998 the *Evening Standard* published a swingeing attack on Diana by George Walden, self-appointed guardian of the public's mental stability, who decried her "wilfulness and self-indulgence", and accused the countless millions of people around the world who had mourned her for their mass hysteria.

"One day," he huffed, "we shall bring ourselves to confront the reality about the late Princess and listen to the voice of reason."

A day or two later, the *Standard* was good enough to publish a letter I wrote in the lady's defence:

So Princess Diana is now arraigned as a symbol of a 'fake' Britain. What, pray, is the 'real' Britain? A land of inhibited citizens and rigid class structures in which no right-thinking princess would ever seek out — let alone comfort, touch or stay in touch with — the ill, the poor and the dispossessed?

Diana's efforts on behalf of those less privileged than herself are a living reproach to the inflexible institutions and their custodians who continue, even now, to deride her.

The British people know a good 'un when they see one. Try telling the millions who mourned her last September that their emotions were 'fake'!

M.J.

13

Shielding
the flame (iii)

O NE AFTERNOON in the spring of 1998 I opened my front door just in time to see a vision of long blonde hair, leopard prints and chiffon scarves cycling past the house. It was Nesta Wyn Ellis. She immediately applied the brakes, flashed her kilowatt smile, stepped down off her bike and came over to greet me.

"How clever of you to open your door just as I was passing! You're just the person to help me with something."

Now Nesta looks like a Nordic Queen or high priestess of Atlantis who has slalomed down into the twentieth century; and when she says could you possibly help her, you tend to jump to attention and say, "Yes, ma'am!"

A week or so before, she had told me that Spirit had asked her to put together a small, free concert or recital with absolutely no publicity or hype. Its purpose? To bring all the controversy and arguments that continued to rage round Princess Diana's name into an atmosphere of harmony and reconciliation.

I suggested that St James's Church in Piccadilly might be a suitable venue, and that is where the recital took place.

Over a cup of tea, she explained why she had been cycling past my door:

"Last night I had five dreams of Diana, and in each of them she was in some distress. In the last dream, she was bandaged from head to toe, and could hardly speak. I said, 'Surely you're being healed here?'

"I was then made to understand that the huge residual wave of grief being directed at her by well-wishers on Earth, and now the latest spate of attacks on her that had just appeared in the British press, were slowing down the healing process.

"In my meditation this morning, I was shown that Diana needed healing from *here*, from Earth, and that this was urgent, because she has to be ready to play her own part in all the great work that is to be done in her name – and that the time for this is coming very close.

"In the last dream I asked her, 'Why do you want *me* to help you?' And again she let me know that, because of my own healing work, which is partly done through music, and through my connection with public figures around the world, I could bring the energies together very quickly.

"In that same dream I brought a man to help heal her, because a man and a woman working together are like the two poles of a magnet, and the healing is stronger. When I woke up, I thought of *you*. I think you're the right person to help me with this assignment."

"I was on my way to Regent's Park, to ask my guides for clarification of what I was to do," she continued, "and there you were right in front of me! So you *must* be the right person to help."

"Whereabouts in Regent's Park?" I asked.

"By a rather special fountain, where there's a powerful ley line with healing force. I can hear them so much more clearly when I'm there."

I was amazed. "That's only twenty yards or so from the seat where I ask Merlin to help me when I get in trouble with my writing!"

We agreed that the fountain would be the perfect place to do the healing, and I said I'd give some thought to what we should do when we got there.

The following Saturday afternoon, as we walked past the lake on our way to the fountain, the tulip beds were almost fluorescent in the dazzling sunlight. Nesta asked me what I thought we should do.

"Why don't we build a crystal octahedron round Diana," I said, "by bringing together two crystal pyramids, one from above and the other from below, which when joined together will accept only positive thoughts and energies reaching her from Earth, and will filter out all the other stuff."

Nesta agreed that protection from negative energy was of prime importance. Then she pointed out that the Park was full of people, and added, "I think we should channel their heart energy, to amplify the healing."

But when we arrived at the fountain, there were very few people about – just one woman asleep on a seat and, behind a tall hedge, a small group lying on the lawn of an adjacent garden.

Nesta said she would concentrate on channelling healing light and love and sending it to Diana, and I decided to visualise the crystal pyramids. We took our places to the east and west of the circular fountain basin, closed our eyes and went to work.

I immediately 'saw' the octahedron taking shape round Diana, but she herself was veiled, indistinct, almost out of focus. As expected, she was wearing a simple white shift.

A slight sound behind me disturbed my concentration. I opened my eyes. Twenty yards away, Nesta was staring past me in disbelief. I turned round. *About forty people had quietly gathered behind me*: a number of French tourists, a Moslem family group and other visitors, all smiling happily as they took part in whatever we were doing.

And behind Nesta, a cheerful Caribbean wedding party was gathering. Around the fountain itself, several Japanese, American and English people were also smiling at us.

We smiled back at them all then resumed our work.

We sensed that, although Diana was grateful for all the love that had been sent to her by people around the world, the waves of grief, yearning and regret still being projected at her were creating an emotional quicksand from which she was finding it very difficult to extract herself.

A few moments later I opened my eyes, turned round. *There was no-one behind me.* And no-one behind Nesta, either!

I rejoined her on her side of the fountain. She reported that Diana was looking her radiant self again.

"I could feel all this joy being sent to her, and being received by her," she said. "After all the grief that has been poured over her, and is *still* being directed at her, joy is the perfect antidote."

She then started speaking to some unseen person in Welsh. When she had finished, she said, "That was Merlin. He seems rather pleased."

"Good," I replied. The entire operation had his hallmarks all over it.

We said goodbye to the swans, geese and wildfowl and left the Park.

14

Heart-to-heart

DURING THE SUMMER of 1998, while sitting with Peter Quiller in his small, overgrown garden in Hertfordshire, I once again consulted the Magician. Here is a fragment of our conversation:

MJ

Diana's departure awoke the heart of this nation, and of many other countries around the world. Was that her role – to demonstrate that the power of the heart is the greatest power of all?

Merlin

Oh indeed yes. And because the heart had been broken, those momentous days were even more emotional than anyone could have expected, and touched people to the very depths of their being.

MJ

Were these events a warning, too? That if we lose our heart, lose our compassion, we ourselves are lost?

Merlin

Oh yes. Princess Diana's incarnation was of the highest importance – it cannot be overstressed just how important. You will have noticed a very negative attitude emerging towards her in recent days, but ignore this: it was bound to happen – a negative backlash, after all the positive energy generated at the time of her departure.

MJ

As you know, I was privileged to be in the Abbey on that day. As the coffin was carried into the Transept, I closed my eyes and got the distinct impression that the Angel of the Presence was in the building.

Merlin

Indeed she was. For what purpose, do you suppose?

MJ

To signify that what was happening was not merely an affair of State, but of significance for the whole world?

Merlin

[*nods*]
It was but a rehearsal.

MJ

[*Yes!*]
A rehearsal? What for?

Merlin

For a day when *all the world* will be thinking the same thoughts. It has never happened, but it will happen soon.

MJ

This is wonderful news, Merlin!

Merlin

And why were *you* in the Abbey on that day?

MJ

A lucky chance?

Merlin

[*shakes his head*]

Nothing happens by chance. Not in *your* life, anyway. I thought you would have realised that by now.

No, you were there because you are one of the guardians of Excalibur, which had to be carried into the Abbey, and withdrawn, and *used*. And used it most certainly was!

MJ

By her brother?

Merlin

By her brother. The crowds outside recognised it at once. Hence that huge wave of applause, which burst through the west door and flooded the Abbey.

MJ

Was her death the price she had to pay for greatness?

Merlin

She had already achieved greatness. Britain and the world had to be reminded that the true power is spiritual, not material. And Diana finally proved it – in the days immediately following her demise, she wielded more power than anyone has ever wielded on Earth. For all her frailties, she triumphantly accomplished the first phase of her mission, which was to—

MJ

Forgive me – the *first* phase?! You mean there's a second?

Merlin

I can hardly believe you asked that question.

MJ

But don't you see – you've just answered a prayer that's been in my heart and mind for over thirty years!

Merlin

Well why did you think I came here today?
   To have a cup of tea and talk over old times?
   [*he shakes his head again*]
Her energy will be re-emerging soon, on many different levels.
And she herself will reappear, with a vital message for the world.
And when she does, her detractors will have much to reconsider.

MJ

She always did want to be an Ambassador! And soon – thank God – it seems that her wish is to be granted! Will there be others?

Merlin

Oh there will be others. Many others. But Diana will be in the vanguard.

MJ

Alleluiah, is all I can say to that!

Merlin

As you would say: "Laugh this one off, brother."

MJ

When the tears have dried, we shall *all* laugh it off.

15

Rehearsal

It is your destiny, one day, to join us.
One day, like us, you will guide younger worlds.
And so it goes on, in a perfect spiral . . .

Merlin
1978

A DREAM, early in November 1998: I am in a long conference chamber, sitting at a mahogany table opposite Diana, who is flanked by four advisers. I am talking intensely, describing in some detail the sheer weight of crisis, tragedy and horror that has led to the moment when – it seems increasingly clear to me – the two worlds must meet. Occasionally, one or other of my listeners nods, but none of them speaks. I sense that I am not a supplicant, but more of a spokesman or advocate.

I then get up and walk the length of the chamber. Only one person is waiting for me: Prince Charles, who is in his shirtsleeves and looking more than a little bewildered and uncertain.

We shake hands. He doesn't speak, so I decide to do so:

"Sir, what is being prepared has been designed to lift not only Britain and its peoples and institutions, but *all* nations and *all* peoples. The greatest care has been taken to ensure that *everyone* will benefit from what is about to happen. Even the power-mongers, tyrants and dictators who are holding their countries to ransom will gain as much by releasing their people as their people will gain from being released.

The Prince nods, then he and I leave the chamber and walk out into the garden. I summon whatever eloquence I can to reassure him, as he is still clearly bemused.

Finally, he seems convinced – or if not convinced, less troubled than a few moments ago. We embrace briefly, and go our separate ways.

16

The Angel

O N A COLD, rain-lashed, wind-swept October afternoon in 1999, Peter Quiller and I drove to the Malvern Hills in the west of England, to making a short video, *The Guardian*. When we had finished, Peter suggested I have a private word with Diana.

I climbed a path through the woods and found myself in a small field near the summit of Ragged Stone hill. A number of rabbits sat up, sniffed at the intruder then hopped away for the cover of the hedges.

In the middle of the field was the sawn-off stump of a tree that had been well over a hundred years old, judging by its rings. I stood on it, closed my eyes and asked Diana if there was anything she wanted to tell us.

About two minutes later, I was told to look up at the sky.

And there it all was – a detailed tableau, created out of cloud of various colours and textures:

At the bottom of this huge cloudscape was all the chaos and darkness of the modern world, with its crises, tragedies and conflicts; rising above that was a hill, very like Ragged Stone hill itself, with a small group of people gathered on its summit; and above them, a huge, white-robed angel which, as I watched, slowly descended until the bottom of its robe obscured the group on the summit.

"Thank you," I said out loud. And then once again, more intensely this time: "*Thank* you!"

So all the years of work were going to pay off, after all! *"Nothing is wasted,"* as Merlin always says . . .

I jumped down off the stump and left the field.

Just before I re-entered the wood, I turned and looked up at the sky.

The tableau had completely disappeared.

I hurried back to PQ, to tell him what I had been shown.

He was pleased, but not the least surprised.

We gathered up our camera bag and other equipment, and set off downhill towards an abandoned stone quarry, where he had parked the car.

"She'll be back," he had said only a few days before, as we sat in the shadow of the giant oak tree in his overgrown garden in Hertfordshire. "But before that happens, the ground must be prepared. I think she'll contact you privately before making any major moves."

"Me?" I said, astounded. "What have *I* got to do with it?"

"But first, you've got work to do," he went on. "You've got to let her come closer. Much closer. *Enjoy* her."

I nodded, as if I knew what he was talking about, but I didn't. I was out of my depth here and out of my class — a Mini trying to keep up with a Ferrari.

Two whole years were to elapse before the penny finally dropped. I think what he had meant, but was too tactful to say outright, was:

"Look, I know you respect, admire and love her — but you do tend to put her on a pedestal. She's not *comfortable* up there! She'd much rather walk arm-in-arm with you and have a good laugh, than endure all that up-on-a-pedestal nonsense. Come on! Remember Ava in *One Touch Of Venus*? It was exactly the same for Robert Walker, when he kissed the statue of the goddess and she immediately came to life — and *thanked him for rescuing her* . . ."

17

Damage limitation (ii)

ON AUGUST 30, 2000, to mark the third anniversary of Diana's death, the *Evening Standard* published yet another two pages of vitriol by George Walden, who not only savaged Diana once again, but this time lashed out at anyone and everyone he could think of, for their "slavish" and "infantile" behaviour three years previously:

> *"Instead of calling the public to order, as any élite worthy of the name would have done, the Government, the media and business urged them on in the biggest, the longest, the most abject and demeaning orgy of lachrymation the country has ever seen."*

"Calling the public to order"?!

What breathtaking arrogance and presumption!

And how would you go about that, mein Obergruppen-führer? By filling the streets with squads of jack-booted, truncheon-wielding storm-troopers? Arresting anyone caught with tears in their eyes? Hurling them into prison and interrogating them?

The British people can count themselves very fortunate indeed that Mr Walden — twenty years in the Foreign Office, a former Minister for Higher Education — never rose to become Home Secretary or even, perish the thought, Prime Minister.

Once again I took my pen out of its scabbard and dashed to her, and our, defence. I was not alone: several other outraged members of the public had written to the *Standard*, and our letters appeared under a banner headline, **Readers defend Diana**.

I had the honour of firing the first salvo:

"George Walden's latest attack on Diana, the late Princess of Wales is, ironically, one of the most devastating self-portraits I have ever read. It reveals a man devoid of perspective, insight, humility, compassion and understanding.

"By impugning Diana for being 'common, cunning, self-centred and under-educated', and then castigating the Government of the day, the media, business, the Church and the British public for the 'orgy' of grief that followed her death, he reveals far more about himself than he does about her or us — none of it very pleasant.

"When 2.5 billion people mourn someone, we must look a little further than the personality of that person. Long before she died, Diana had become an archetype. She represented something far more than herself or even her sex. For all her faults — which she ruefully acknowledged — she had become a champion of certain abiding truths which people all round the world immediately recognised and saluted.

"They also saluted her brother, who had the temerity to say, during his historic tribute to her in Westminster Abbey:

"I don't think she ever understood why her genuinely good intentions were sneered at by the media — why there appeared to be a permanent quest on their behalf to bring her down. My own and only explanation is that genuine goodness is threatening to those at the opposite end of the moral spectrum."

M.J.

18

The Human Family

A Vision of the Peoples of the World

THIS DRAFT *Declaration is dedicated to Diana, the much-loved late Princess of Wales whose life, work and example inspired it. It is an attempt to put into words what she is undoubtedly wishing for us all — and what she would probably try to implement, if she were authorised and empowered to do so.*

She was both ill-prepared and ill-equipped for her mission; she had her frailties and shortcomings — which she cheerfully acknowledged; she attracted more than her fair share of critics and detractors. Yet somehow she surmounted every obstacle in her path and, when her life here ended, enjoyed her greatest triumph:

She reached the hearts and minds of some 2.5 billion people — almost a third of the population of the world — which is more than anyone has ever reached, before or since.

Preamble

Despite the best efforts of all those who work ceaselessly for peace and harmony, and despite the deep reservoirs of tolerance and goodwill that exist among us, the nations and peoples of the world remain disunited. Maybe this is inevitable, given that the human race comprises so many different races, each with its own character and culture, each rich in history, traditions and ideals, and each possessed of a fierce, and justifiable, pride in itself.

And yet the problems of the world will only be solved if we put aside our differences and begin to think as *one* people, *one* race, *one* family. If we cannot yet find a unity of outlook and perspective, at least we can create a code of honour or mission statement for the whole human race as we step into the future together.

So long as we remain without one, we have no voice, no accepted standards, principles or ethics to guide us – and little to protect us from despots, dictators and other public figures who might be tempted to abuse their power.

Someone once said, "Every nation has its own particular genius, and has something unique to offer the world." That is as true today as it ever was – so let us determine to resolve our differences, once and for all – by announcing to the world at large what we believe, and by recognising how much we have to gain by codifying our relationship with each other.

The Human Family

A Vision of the Peoples of the World

We, the peoples of the world, having just stepped into the future – the uncharted territory of a new century and a new Millennium – have already made two momentous discoveries. The first is that we are members of one human family sharing a single planet. The second is that we not only have the right but also the power and the means to change the world we live in for the better. These two discoveries are among the most important we have ever made. They can literally shape our lives, and guide and inspire us as we embark on the next phase of the great adventure.

A brief summary of our beliefs and intentions now follows:

We believe

. . . that our past has much to teach us, and that we can learn as much, or more, from our mistakes as we can from our successes;

. . . that by acknowledging those mistakes, we can prepare the way for reconciliations and renewed friendships between us;

. . . that our differences of nationality, culture and history are a source of the richness of human society;

. . . that tolerance and open-mindedness, backed up by positive action, can heal most of the wounds we have inflicted on each other;

. . . that we are all entitled to our beliefs, customs and preferences – but we have no right to impose those beliefs, customs and preferences on others;

. . . that the primary purpose of education from now on should be to encourage and empower the personal growth of every student, and to eliminate fear, arrogance and aggression from the syllabus once and for all;

. . . that competition is healthy only so long as it does not lead to ruthlessness, dishonesty and unscrupulousness;

. . . that honour, respect, kindness and compassion should no longer be thought of as virtues, but rather as an essential part of our nature, without which we are incomplete;

. . . that our governments should reflect the will of the people they serve; that they should guide, advise and lead us – but not compel or attempt to control us;

. . . that men and women have much to learn from each other, and good reason to respect each other; and that they make better partners and colleagues than rivals;

. . . that in all matters affecting the quality of our lives and our future, men, women and children should all have an equal voice;

. . . and that, in view of the interconnectedness of all people and all things, we should now consider ourselves to be citizens not only of our country and our race, but of the world.

We intend

. . . to face the future with confidence and self-respect, but without arrogance or insularity;

. . . to share our knowledge and experience, our strengths and resources with others;

. . . to remember that in all our encounters and relationships, we are not only representing ourselves, but our family, our country and our race;

. . . to contribute whatever we can to the quality of human life;

. . . to do whatever we can to protect the Earth, whose gifts we have taken for granted and whose hospitality we have abused;

. . . to do whatever we can to create, and to help others to create, another way of life on Earth – a life without poverty, disease, crime, famine, fear, injustice, oppression, insecurity, hatred and war.

And who is going to perform this miracle?

We are . . .

The Human Family

A Vision of the Peoples of the World

The above draft has no author – it wrote itself because it wanted to do so. Like any first draft it is incomplete, its purpose being to prompt others to create and publish a more evolved and complete

Vision of the Peoples of the World — an informal code of honour and practice that will set the seal on our lives and on human relations for generations to come.

We urge those who are privileged to draw up this document to do so in a language that will be understood by us all — especially our children.

As **The Human Family** is intended merely as an expression of certain universal ideals, rather than as a proposed treaty or some other instrument that would require official ratification, it is submitted for no more than the general assent and approval-in-principle of the Members of the United Nations.

The Human Family was broadcast on Christmas Day 2000 on BBC Radio 2 in London, and again on Thursday, 8 February. Hundreds of e-mails were sent in by listeners to Johnnie Walker and myself, all of them endorsing the project in the strongest possible terms.

At the suggestion of the UN Secretary-General's office in New York, a transcript of **The Human Family** has been sent to the United Kingdom's Permanent Mission to the United Nations, for submission to the UN General Assembly; and following the suggestion of Radio 2 listeners, I have also sent it to the Model UN (young people's UN in The Hague) and to the Secretary-General of the British Commonwealth at Marlborough House, St James's.

It is simply a matter of sowing the seed wherever we can, and hoping it falls on fertile soil . . .

Johnnie,
This is my first e-mail to you.
I was so knocked out by that Declaration —
it was truly wonderful and uplifting.
I am sure that today you are going to receive thousands
of e-mails, and I would describe the words coming through
as something similar to the first broadcast of H G Wells'
War Of The Worlds on radio in the United States.

Anyone who heard this today is going to be talking
about it and wanting to find out more.
I really think that today you may have changed the world.
Well done, Johnnie – you may have inspired people
to go out and make those words a reality.

Rose-Marie McGinn
8 February, 2001

From: Peter B Corrin
Subject: Johnnie Walker Show
Date 08 February '01

Johnnie,

I never miss a show on my weekly run back from Bristol to
Leicestershire – too much good music, great guests and, of
course, Sal's invaluable information – but last night's interview
with Michael Joseph literally stopped me in my tracks: I had to pull
off the M5 (the only moving motorway last night), park up and just
listen. I missed the Christmas day programme, but that monologue
left me stunned.

Where has this chap been hiding? Why is he not Minister of
Education, and why oh why has no-one been listening to him for
the last 25 years? I cannot remember when I last heard so much
sense in 20 minutes.

Education in this country effectively stopped in the late '60s,
and since then, we as a nation have screwed up the lives of millions
for generations to come, because uneducated, disempowered
children become uneducated, disempowered people who cannot
bring their children up to be any better because they don't *know*
any better. And the schools are out of control and chasing short-
term rainbows, so the horror becomes compounded.

'Dumbing down' is terrifyingly real: this country is turning out an endless procession of under-educated, ignorant, angry, frustrated and resentful children every year – and then expecting more of them in their working lives!

If you don't believe this, stand for five minutes on any street corner in the UK and listen to the speech the people under 30 use: it is disrespectful, slurred, mispronounced, cliché-ridden and redolent of the lowest common denominator. Our teachers are as frustrated as the kids they are trying to teach – and at the centre of all of it is a rotten education system.

Sorry to sound off, but Michael struck a chord with me. Where can I contact him to find out more about his work, his books and his crusade?

Many thanks for your version of public service broadcasting. Keep it up! While there are broadcasters like you, willing to devote time to people like this, there is still some hope left.

Maybe I'll even begin to believe in the BBC again!
Love to Sal and many thanks again,

Peter Corrin
pbcorrin@lanternltd.co.uk

19

Dear Prince William . . .

01.01.01
HRH The Prince William
St James's Palace

Dear Prince William,

The Human Family: A Vision of the Peoples of the World

Further to my letter of 19 December: with all the calls on your time and attention on Christmas day, I very much doubt if you had a chance to listen to the end of Johnnie Walker's show on Radio 2, when he broadcast **The Human Family** for the first time. But a nephew of mine has since given me a mini-CD of it, including Johnnie Walker's introduction, during which he mentioned that **The Human Family** is dedicated to Diana, Princess of Wales.

I am therefore enclosing a cassette copy of this part of the broadcast, and also a copy of the complete written version, as it appears in a book I am currently writing.

You might care to know that **The Human Family** started out as something else altogether. In view of the disintegration of standards and ideals that goes on every day – we seem to be living at a time when greed and selfishness are instantly rewarded, and courtesy and kindness are regarded as some kind of weakness – I have long thought it deplorable that we have no written Constitution in these islands.

So, in sheer frustration, last summer I drafted one – or should I say it wrote itself. Everyone I showed it to loved it, which encouraged me to send it to the editors of all the broadsheets and Sunday papers. Half of them didn't even trouble to reply; the rest said, "No thanks."

Undeterred, I sent it to the Prime Minister, who passed it on to the Home Office – and I received a letter saying, "There is no need for a British Constitution". I called the Home Office and asked my correspondent who had made this historic decision on our behalf.

"The Government," she said, as if that ended the matter.

"The Government comprises a number of individuals," I replied. "Who made this decision – and when, and where?"

"I don't have to answer these questions!" the woman almost shouted – then slammed the phone down.

I confess I was rather angry for a few moments – but was soon far too busy to remain so: it had just occurred to me that the human race has no written Constitution or code of honour either! So I made a few adjustments to **A British Constitution**, and it turned effortlessly into **The Human Family: A Constitution for the Peoples of the World** – which I sent at once to a friend, Jean Hudon, in Quebec. He wisely suggested I should re-title it, as a Constitution would need to be ratified, and might get bogged down in all kinds of legal tangles. He suggested that it should be more of a mission statement, so I altered its name accordingly.

It is no secret that Prince Charles has a heartfelt desire to put the 'Great' back in Britain, to halt the decline in so many areas of the nation's life. The nature of much of his public work suggests that this is indeed one of his very highest priorities.

But this dream of his – which all of us who love this land must share – will never be realised so long as arrogant politicians and blinkered bureaucrats continue to disregard the public they were elected or employed to serve – and to treat with contempt any idea, however timely, urgent or vital, that they themselves didn't think of first.

Never mind: I am given to understand by inner sources that, despite her new role as part of the European Economic Community, Britain *will* return to pre-eminence – not the kind of pre-eminence and power she enjoyed at the height of the Empire, perhaps, but another, equally important kind: I am told that, given the will and the heart to do so by those who care deeply enough about her, Britain *can* become a beacon of light as the world moves into the new century and the new Millennium – as a living example of honour, wisdom, experience and compassion.

It is for this reason that I firmly believe that we in these islands could only benefit from a written Constitution or code of honour. What is *any* man without a code of honour and practice?! And what is any nation?

If you happen to agree, then I shall be greatly honoured if you and Prince Charles will use the enclosed as a preliminary rough sketch, and then do whatever you think fit – with the assistance of anyone you choose – to re-draft it into a workable British Constitution.

The very first edit might be to change *"We, the peoples of the world . . ."* back to *"We, the peoples of the British Isles . . ."* which is how this Declaration began in the first place.

Judging by the enthusiastic reaction of many listeners to Johnnie Walker's Christmas programme (total strangers, I hasten to add, and not just my own chums) the project will be enthusiastically welcomed and supported by the British people as a whole.

Please accept my renewed best wishes for the coming year – and for all the years to come.

Yours respectfully,
Michael Joseph

20

Sir . . .

*Britain . . . a country once noted for being
law-abiding, tolerant and benign, has become —
as a matter of statistical fact — the most drink-sodden,
drug-soaked, poorly educated, promiscuous
nation in western Europe, with rates of
theft and violent crime that are fast
outstripping those of the USA.*

David Thomas
Telegraph Magazine

11 July, 2001
HRH The Prince of Wales KG
St James's Palace
SW1A 1BS

Sir,
The Human Family: A Vision of the Peoples of the World
   At the beginning of the year I sent a transcript of **The Human
Family** to Prince William, suggesting that he and you might like
to use it as a template, as it were, for the creation of a written
Constitution for the United Kingdom. (*Please see the enclosed copy of
my letter to Prince William, and a transcript of* **The Human Family**.)
   To my astonishment, I received no reply whatsoever. I can only

assume that whoever saw my letter and enclosures considered them to be unsuitable. Yet I can hardly believe that anyone in St James's Palace considers that 'the Matter of Britain' is an inappropriate topic to set before Prince William and yourself.

Maybe someone thought, "He isn't a Government minister or senior civil servant, so what right does *he* have to propose a Constitution?"

I would respectfully suggest that *anyone* who loves his country, and is grateful for what his country has given him, is entitled to do so. A nation with no written code of honour is ripe for decay, disintegration and anarchy.

If no-one believes in anything any more, if self-respect and respect for others are now 'old hat', then we are in big trouble.

Someone has to take the lead here – and I still hope that you and Prince William will do so. You could leave Britain no finer legacy than a code of honour that will set the tone in these islands – and further afield – for years to come.

Judging by the extraordinary response to **The Human Family** by listeners to BBC Radio 2 – who heard it last Christmas, and again in early February – it is a project that would enjoy widespread popular support – especially if, when it is first announced, the public are invited to send in their own thoughts, suggestions and ideas.

Meanwhile, at the suggestion of Mr Kofi Annan's office in New York, I have submitted **The Human Family** to the UK's Permanent Secretary to the UN, in the hope that this project will be presented to the UN General Assembly for its approval.

I have the honour to remain Your Royal Highness's humble and obedient servant,

Michael Joseph
Enclosures

Eventually I received a reply from Prince Charles's office, saying that there was no record of my having sent any letters to Prince William. Which I found rather odd, as I had delivered them both by hand to the duty officer at the gates of St James's Palace.

Prince Charles kindly sent his 'best wishes' but, to my astonishment – but *not* to that of my more cynical friends – in his letter he made no reference whatsoever to **The Human Family**, or to my invitation . . .

PART 3

Our Book

*For young people everywhere —
because you are the future*

DIANA REPORTS THAT, soon after she and Dodi 'got home' – and they had recovered from the shock and violence of their sudden arrival – she consulted planetary records as she wanted to confirm reports that, during the second half of the last century, children all over the 'civilised' world, so-called, became more and more involved in crime or anti-social behaviour of one kind or another – from truancy, petty larceny, and physical and verbal abuse to destruction of property, arson, torture and murder.

She also discovered the cause:

They were following our example. They were absorbing the news every day – and the violent, often horrific movies and television programmes we create for our own amusement. They were playing the mindless, destructive, hyperactive computer games we create for theirs.

A while later she visited a 'creative action' group attended by kids whose criminal activities had shortened their own lives. During their discussions, an idea was born. Diana has asked me to stress that this idea came from the kids – and not from her:

"If adults don't seem to be able to run life on Earth without endless hostility and aggression and war, why don't *we* put together a simple handbook for kids everywhere? Something that'll help the next generation to live in comparative peace and quiet – without blowing each other to bits!"

What follows is the first draft of that document . . .

Introduction

JUST ONE THING before we start:
'Our' Book doesn't mean yours and mine – it means **your** book.

It's yours, it belongs to **you**, to all young people. And you can add to it in any way you want, to improve and enlarge it. And if kids everywhere do the same, and you synthesise the results, you'll end up with an amazing document – a simple guidebook that will spare future generations from having to endure all the hassles and heartaches **you've** had to contend with.

You might think some of the following ideas and suggestions are a bit too simple and too obvious to deserve a place in this book – but what's simple and obvious to **you** might not be to everyone else, so please be patient and don't throw them out. Well not yet, anyway!

For example: *"Be kind."*

Your immediate reaction to that one will probably be, "Oh come on, lady – what's new about **that**?!" Nothing new at all. But how many people do you know who **are** kind?

Are **you**?!

Can you imagine how many boys – who like to be thought of as tough, and who can blame them? – think that kindness is for wimps and weaklings?

If only they knew!

If only they knew how much respect they'd get from everyone if they **were** kind, if they used their strength and dynamic personalities to **protect** the people around them – especially younger and more defenceless kids.

From 'heavy' to hero in one move! That can't be bad.

It's simple logic, really – if everyone understood and accepted those two words, and acted accordingly, there'd be no need for this or any other guidebook! **And most human problems wouldn't even exist!**

It might be quite a while before we get there, so the sooner we make a start, the better . . . Good luck!

Ambition

Ambition is the goal. And if you can reach the goal and score without carving anyone up on the way, you're a winner . . .

Apologising

"I was wrong. I'm sorry."

What an amazing amount of pain and aggravation we could save ourselves, if only we had the courage to **admit it** when we're in the wrong! Unfortunately, most of us refuse to – we dig in our heels, and so does the other person, and the situation gets worse by the minute.

It also happens at the international level too, when neither side is prepared to back down. And so the feuds go on, sometimes for centuries, and even, in a few notorious cases, for **thousands of years** – with each new generation being taught to hate, and to keep the vendetta alive.

Most confrontations could be defused if both parties were willing to listen to each other's grievances, and to work out a plan that everybody can live with . . .

Bullies

Bullies are frightened people, who lash out to hide their fear. They have cronies, but no real friends. My own personal message to them is this:

"You obviously have a powerful personality, and physical strength to back it up. Why not try **sharing** that strength with the kids around you, rather than imposing it on them? Using it **for** them, rather than against them? Chances are, you'll end up a star, a leader, liked and admired by everyone, rather than feared and hated . . ."

Compassion

Be aware other people's distress, and if you're in a position to help – and **if** they agree – do what you can for them.

If you're only concerned about your **own** welfare and peace of mind, can you really expect them to come running when **you're** in trouble?!

Compliments

Don't be afraid to dish out compliments if you think they're deserved.

And if someone compliments **you**, never think of those compliments as if they're tributes from your inferiors. You don't **have** any inferiors! No-one does . . .

Confidence

Confidence doesn't have to boast about itself. Real confidence is a kind of quiet inner strength that will draw other people to you like a magnet.

And if you've got enough of it to help develop the confidence of the people around you, your star will begin to shine . . .

Consequences

"What goes round, comes round," as the saying goes. It simply means that whatever we think, do and say has a habit of returning to us. So be careful what you think, do and say – because if it's negative or destructive, eventually it'll boomerang on you – and **nothing can stop it**, because it's part of the Universal law . . .

Courage

Life is tough. In a lot of ways it's a survival course, without instructions. If you can tough it out – keep going, whatever they throw at you – you've got courage, and that's something **no-one** can take away from you . . .

Courtesy

Treat other people with respect – and you'll probably have theirs in return . . .

Cruelty

Cruel people are in some kind of pain, so they tend to share it, to spread it around, rather than examine the cause of their pain. And to do so, they choose weaker, defenceless people – or animals – as their victims, which makes them cowards as well . . .

Dreams

Trust your dreams: they are your passport to the inner worlds. When we live in the physical world, we are *not* confined to it . . .

Encouragement

It doesn't cost anything. It only takes a little time. So how about encouraging someone you know to finish something they've started? It can be something small – or something as big as their career, their entire future!

Fame

Most people want to be rich or famous, or both. No doubt about it, money can be very useful, but fame?! Take my word for it, fame is a poisoned chalice.

It promises so much – and it robs you blind. It's the end of your privacy, the end of your private life. Become famous and, whether you want to or not, you immediately become food for gossip, a curiosity, a freak, public property. You also become the subject of a hundred million desires and fantasies, prejudices and hates.

Still not convinced?! Still want to live your life in the glare of the spotlight, under the microscope – a thing, a laboratory specimen, no longer a person entitled to privacy? Then don't let *me* stand in your way. But don't say you haven't been warned . . .

Forgiving

To forgive someone is to halve the problem. To hit back at them is to double it . . .

Friends

Our real friends are more valuable than diamonds or gold. They make a huge contribution to our sense of identity and our confidence. They are always there for us when the flak starts flying.

Friends should never be taken for granted – make sure you give **them** the time and thought and care that they give **you** . . .

Giving something back

When we're young, almost everything is given to us – our food, our clothes, somewhere to live and, if we're lucky, books, toys and pocket-money too. We take it for granted that our parents or someone else is going to supply whatever we need.

So when we get older, we have to **learn** how to give! Which can be very difficult for kids who have been spoiled by their parents, and have never gone without. *And* for those who were given little or nothing . . .

One of the ways of giving is simply to **think** about other people – what they might need, what might help them or please them. This is the beginning of growing up . . .

Gossip

Gossip is fun, and most of us do it. But taken too far, dishing the dirt can ruin other people's careers, reputations and – if it gets out of hand – even their lives . . .

Honesty

We can cheat other people, but we can't cheat ourselves. Somewhere, deep down, we always know if we're being honest or not. We might pretend to be glad we've cheated – but self-respect can't be built out of lies . . .

Hope

Hope is a torch that keeps the darkness at bay. Always carry one, wherever you go!

Kindness

"Be kind."

Even if you're tempted not to be. Even though someone is cruel to you. Because if you hit back – as I so often did – you'll **both** be in the wrong . . .

Loneliness

We all feel lonely at times. That's the time to call a friend, and tell them you just want to talk. (Okay, so that sounds like a commercial for the phone company. So sue me . . . J)

Love

Love is a form of magic. It changes everyone and everything it touches. It can mend all kinds of things that are broken. It can build all kinds of things that weren't there before. It creates partnerships, families, dynasties. It can even turn enemies into friends – and there's no greater magic than that . . .

Loyalty

Have you ever stood by someone when everyone else was attacking them? You might get caught in the crossfire – but stand your ground. One day, when the flak is flying in **your** direction, you might be very grateful to have someone stand by **you** like that . . .

Manners

Good manners are out of fashion. **Big** mistake! They are the cement that holds human society together. Take a good look round. Without good manners – which is another way of saying tolerance, politeness and consideration – civilisation itself is now falling apart at the seams . . .

Never give up

For most people, life's a bitch – day after day of drudgery or insecurity, loneliness or fear. But hang in there – the longer you hold out, the bigger the chance that eventually it'll all turn round . . .

Originality

Our individuality is our most precious possession – much more valuable than diamonds. Don't resent other people because they're different from you, or because they look and sound and act differently, and have different beliefs and customs. What a terrible world it would be if we all went round like cyborgs or robots, moving and sounding exactly like each other.

Pain

There's not only physical pain, there's mental and emotional pain too. And there's far too much of it in the world, so we're all faced with a simple choice:

Am I going to hurt the people round me? Or am I going to do what I can to make life less painful for them? In other words, am I going to be part of the problem, or part of the solution?

Punctuality

Keeping other people waiting is a sign of disrespect. Do **you** like being kept waiting? Probably not. Nobody does . . .

Revenge

Forget about getting your revenge – you don't have to do a thing – the person who's hurt or insulted you will get their comeuppance in the end. It's called karma . . . (*see* **Consequences**)

Selfishness

Being selfish is a *very* lonely business . . .

The Truth

The Truth is bigger than all of us combined. The Truth is what has actually happened everywhere, and when and where it happened, and why. No-one can possibly know all *that*!

Think for yourself. Explore life. Draw your own conclusions. Never surrender your right to be yourself – because **that's the primary purpose of your life**!

Never tell other people what to think and how to run their lives. By all means offer them your advice if they want it, but always leave them free to decide for themselves . . .

Unselfishness

Unselfishness is a very attractive quality. But not even the best machines can run forever – so remember to give **yourself** some quality time, now and then . . .

Working on ourselves

"Nobody's perfect. I'm not perfect. But I'm working on it!"

We don't come ready-made, like cars and computers – we have to **learn** how to be a person, by watching our parents, our family and friends – and the people around us.

The trick is – copy their best qualities, steer clear of their bad ones, then throw in a few good ones of your own.

Don't be afraid to improve yourself: Go from good to better, then to best . . . Polish that diamond!

Be a **star**!

Go for it!

Y OU MIGHT BE surprised to know that this is probably the very first guidebook that has ever been offered to kids everywhere. Discuss it with your friends – and with your parents and teachers too, if you like. Add everything and anything that you think will improve it. This is only a very crude first draft – imagine what it can become if you **all** add your own ideas to it:

A book of Life!

A few simple ideas that can take most of the pain out of our everyday lives. An entirely new approach to human relationships – no more competing with each other, no more trying to outdo each other.

Imagine a world in which everyone helps everyone else – **and then bring it into reality!** No more loneliness. No more fear. No more cruelty. No more violence.

If that's what you really want, **nothing and nobody can stop you from having it!**

You have the power. So go for it! Change the world!

Because if **you** don't, no-one ever will.

All my love,

Diana

167

PART 4

Envoy

1

Earth Mother

FOR QUITE A while now I have been growing restless, sensing that there's something I have to do — and have been wanting to do ever since I got home. And recently, throughout the year 2000, in fact, this feeling has been growing more and more intense, urgent.

So many wonderful things have happened to me since I got back, and I have been having so many reunions with treasured friends *and* first-time encounters with so many extraordinary people I have long wanted to meet, that it very nearly slipped my mind — I'm ashamed to say! But then, in a quiet moment, I remembered what it was I wanted to do. I tuned in to HQ, and asked for permission to speak with the Earth Mother. The reply came at once:

"We were wondering when we would hear from you, Diana. Yes, of course. Any time." The voice was neither feminine nor masculine, maybe both. I wondered if it might be an angel of some kind.

"Now?" I said — hoping I wasn't pushing my luck.

"It is always now," was the amused reply.

I laughed. Of course it is. "What do I have to do?"

"Close your eyes and just imagine her," said the voice, "and she'll be with you immediately."

I did so — and found myself at the bottom of a huge hollow sphere, miles and miles in diameter, in a dark green landscape with rivers and forests and waterfalls and distant mountains, just like a

Tuscan scene by da Vinci. The terrain itself curved up, up and away in every direction, and melted into the sky, which also curved, darkening from pale summer blue to deep sapphire, crowned by a thousand glittering galaxies above me.

It was the world, *inside out*! I felt like Alice through the Looking Glass. As I got my bearings, I noticed a small green hill to my right, with a ring of trees round its summit. A moment later I was inside this ring of trees — and there She was, sitting on a moss-covered seat, in a gown that shimmered like a dragonfly's wings.

But her face! The perfection of it, the unfathomable wisdom and compassion of it literally took my breath away. But even more than that — the pain she has suffered, the billions of acts of unkindness and cruelty she has endured at our hands, have given her eyes what I can only describe as a terrible beauty, an indefinable holiness.

I fell at her feet, reached out to touch her, and wept. I know I was only experiencing the tiniest fraction of her pain, but even that broke my heart. As the enormity of the sacrifice she has made throughout the ages began to dawn on me, it felt as if my tears were made of fire; I was half-choking, and could hardly breathe. I felt her hand touch my head, and immediately the fire stopped burning, my throat became less constricted. I got up into a kneeling position.

"Forgive us, dear Mother, forgive us," I managed to whisper.

"You are already forgiven," said the Earth.

That did it. Another stream of tears poured down my face. Already forgiven?! How can *anyone* forgive so much?

She waited patiently until I had recovered. I smiled sheepishly at her for making such a spectacle of myself — but I knew that she understood that too.

"You are a good soldier," she said. "One of the very best. You have fought hard, with limited resources, and often thought you had lost." She shook her head. "You haven't lost, my child. You have won a great victory. And in due course you will win others just as great."

I couldn't help myself. I tossed protocol or whatever to the wind, stood up, stepped forward and threw my arms round her.

"It's a great honour to fight for you, dear Mother," I said — when I could speak. Then I broke free, before I disgraced myself with yet another flood of tears, and ran away through the trees, down the hill and back onto the plain . . .

I opened my eyes and found myself back home.

A number of very special friends were waiting for me. As I stood up they approached, smiling, and I melted into their loving embrace.

They already knew.

2

The God Child

And all shall be well
and all manner of things shall be well
when the tongues of flame are enfolded
into the crowned knot of fire
and the fire and the rose are one.

T S Eliot
Salisbury Cathedral

I'M CERTAIN NOW that if my friends hadn't been waiting for me when I got home after meeting the Earth Mother, it would have taken me a long time to recover from the shock and pain of seeing what I saw in her face – for all its beauty and serenity:

As a race, we have almost tortured our own mother to death! Since the beginning, she has fed and clothed and housed us, free of charge – and how have we repaid her? By systematically cutting, burning, raping, poisoning and blowing her up with bombs and explosives.

Were we always like that?

"Of course we were," say the cynics. "It's human nature. It's perfectly normal behaviour – kill or be killed, survival of the fittest – or strongest, or most cunning, or most heavily armed."

I wonder. I have looked into the eyes of thousands of children, and never once seen a murderer or torturer or demon gazing back at me.

174

I believe that, as a race, we have been *trained* to be destroyers, *trained* to suspect other races and religions, *trained* to invade other peoples' lands and kill them, whether or not they put up any resistance. Every Empire in history has been carved out by the sword.

Who *are* the sinister figures behind all this? And *why* have they orchestrated such wholesale horror and bloodshed?

I confess I haven't the slightest idea. And I'm not sure I *want* to know. All I do know is that it has been going on, more or less unchecked, for centuries. Correction – for millennia. Not only do these shadowy characters seem to be intent on treating *us* the way we treat our cattle, they don't seem to be the least bit concerned that the Earth itself might be destroyed in the process.

And that's why, as the year 2000 drew to a close, I decided to go for the big one.

I had already had that short, devastating audience with the Earth herself. So who did I ask to see next? I think you've probably guessed.

It wasn't quite as easy as getting to see the Earth Mother: I was told I'd have to go into retreat for a while, so I did. I was taken to what I can only describe as a white palace or temple on a mountain-top, and shown into the most perfect garden you can imagine.

These things are all symbolic – I think I saw what I *expected* to see, if you follow me. Maybe the place was quite different from what I saw and experienced, but no matter.

It was a place – or maybe I should say dimension – where doubt and fear and pain just can't exist, the vibration is so high. I was utterly at peace there; totally at ease, with no doubt or concern or lingering anxiety – just the blissful realisation that everything is known there, and understood, and is *indestructible*. And that, somehow, even the nightmares we have conjured up, and the appalling pain we have inflicted on ourselves and each other, will eventually end, and we'll get back on course – working *with*, rather than against, the original plan or universal blueprint, the Prime Directive.

And now you're going to have to forgive me. Because there are no words, no pictures, no music and no sounds that can do justice to what happened to me next . . .

I was asleep under a tree rather like a weeping willow, except that instead of leaves, it had cascades of flowers that reached the ground (weren't there trees like that in the *Pastoral Symphony* sequence of *Fantasia*?) when suddenly I woke up.

A girl of about twelve was standing a few feet away, watching me. She smiled and, as She did so, my heart missed a beat.

I knew who She was.

And why She was showing herself to me like this. If She had shown herself in all her glory, I'd have been blinded.

Although She was so young, it was I who felt like a child in her presence. She beckoned, so I got to my feet and went over to her, and we walked for a while in silence. She slid her hand into mine.

And as She did so . . . I had my answers. *All of them.*

Although not a word was spoken between us – there's no need for speech up there: every thought is clearly understood, every question instantly answered – here is what I remember of our wordless conversation:

Diana

Thank you for agreeing to see me, divine Mother.

The God Child

Thank you for never losing sight of me, Diana.

Diana

You know why I'm here.

The God Child

I do.

176

Here we go again – yours truly rushing in as impulsively as ever:

Diana

Enough is enough! There has been too much betrayal, too much pain, too much tragedy, too much torture, too much sacrifice.

A split-second pause before She replied:

The God Child

Indeed there has, Ambassador.

Diana

On behalf of our beloved Mother, Earth, who has loved and protected us unconditionally, despite everything we have done to her; on behalf of all the living creatures we have slaughtered; and on behalf of almost a billion innocent human beings who have been sacrificed, I humbly ask you to intercede without delay.

There was a longer pause this time, before the God Child replied:

The God Child

It is being done.

I almost fainted with relief.

The God Child

The Light and Love and Power that so many have been praying for are already on their way. They have been transmitted to the Central Sun, which is now relaying them to your own Sun which, in turn, is stepping them down before relaying them to Earth.

Soon, all those on Earth who wish to do so will receive as much of this Power as they can absorb. Everything will proceed from *that*.

I woke, and found myself under the willow tree again. Then, despite my excitement, and my impatience to share the news with everyone I know, I fell into a blissful, dreamless sleep, then woke once again — and found myself back home.

An even bigger crowd of friends and loved ones was waiting for me. And *what* a celebration followed!

May something very like it soon be echoing and re-echoing all round the world — the first party *everyone* gets to attend as an honoured guest!

You all deserve it.

I love you. And so does everyone else up here.

See you soon . . .

St. Valentine's day, 2003

I WAS RECENTLY privileged to meet God the Father, no less – and I have to tell you, his power and Light and beauty left me speechless. He appeared as a young man – not as the white-haired, bearded patriarch I'd always imagined him to be.

For a while we gazed at each other in silence. I think my mouth must have been hanging open in awe, because his smile – which contained every emotion I have ever known or imagined, and several more besides – had an unmistakable flicker of amusement in it.

He thanked me – He thanked *me*, would you believe?! – then said: "Honey, you ain't seen nothin' yet. Wait till you meet the boss . . ."

My head was beginning to spin. "If *you're* not the boss," I thought, "then—?"

"My better half," He said simply, reading my mind.

And we both burst out laughing – He because it's just about the most superb joke ever, and I in sheer relief:

God's better half . . . That's the best news this Universe ever had, if you ask me.

Afterword

A N OLD AND trusted friend of mine who has just read this book has written to say that he was surprised by Diana's occasional outspokenness and residual anger. "Surely no-one who has returned to 'the other side' would use the kind of language she does here — especially someone as gentle and compassionate as Diana. So I'm wondering if it is *your* anger and fighting talk, Michael, not hers."

I confess that the very same thought had occurred to me too — and caused me a lot of soul-searching — so I replied as follows:

'Yes, you're so right — she was, and is, a gentle and compassionate being. But what a fighter when there was fighting to be done! What an inventive, cunning, persistent and, on occasion, ruthless fighter to boot (ask her opponents)!

'She was subject to duality as we all are — and in her Kali aspect, boy! could she fight her corner! She *had* to — she was the Princess in the tower, desperate to escape; vilified, demonised, outnumbered and outgunned by the "old guard".

'Escape she did — in a manner that shocked the world. And soon afterwards, the compassion you mention prompted her to review the records of the human race throughout the last century — and when she was confronted by the sheer scale of the death and destruction caused by advanced modern weapons — *and* the staggering number of lives lost to famine and malnutrition — her fury knew no bounds . . .

'Just one glimpse of the roll of more than *a hundred million* sudden (or slow and agonising) deaths of innocent people during the last 100 years was enough to sicken, appal and enrage Diana.

'The mother in her lamented the loss of countless sons and

daughters; and the warrior in her was outraged by the sheer *cowardice* of bullets, shells, mortars, mines, bombs, torpedoes and missiles which can kill hundreds or thousands of people at a time – *without the firer even seeing his victims* . . .

'Channelling is very much a tightrope walk, so I did my best to distinguish between the times that I was merely a stenographer, taking down what *she* wanted to say in her own words – and those when she was relying on me to put her ideas into words.

'But, bearing in mind what you say, I'll go through the book once again, and seek out any glaring examples of, "That's not her talking, Michael – that's *you*."

'Oh, and by the way – Diana made it clear that certain subjects were taboo, so I simply didn't go there: her relationships with Prince Charles and the Royal family, her private life, and so on. Why? Quite simply, because the book is more concerned with the present and the future than with the past.

'PS: When I first started 'tuning in', in 1967, I discovered that there was a lot of 'junk mail' floating around in the astral planes. My instructor said, "Well what do you expect? They're the dumping ground of most of human thought. Not to worry – just rise above them, and soon you'll be flying high."

'And you know what? He was right!'

The Global Consciousness Project

W<small>E DO NOT</small> feel that our minds are isolated within our bodies. In truth, we experience the world with beautiful immediacy, we know our loved ones from afar, and we leap in thought to the stars. Research shows that we may have direct communication links with each other, that intentions can have effects in the world despite physical barriers and separations.

Evidence compels us to consider that consciousness may operate as a nonlocal field. The Global Consciousness Project takes this possibility a step further, proposing that the fields generated by individual consciousness would interact and combine, and ultimately have global dimensions.

Usually, because we are busy with individual lives, there is little to produce structure in the field. But occasionally there are global-scale events that bring great numbers of us to a common focus.

To study the effects, we have created a world-spanning network of detectors sensitive to coherence and resonance in the mental domain. Continuous streams of data are sent over the Internet to be archived and correlated with events that may evoke a world-wide consciousness.

Examples that appear to have done so include the funeral ceremonies of Princess Diana, a few minutes around midnight on any New Year's Eve, the first hour of NATO bombing in Yugoslavia, and earthquakes in Turkey, Central America, India.

http://noosphere.princeton.edu/

Photo-call

07.00 hrs, 24 August 2002

IT IS A SUNNY AFTERNOON, on a wide street with little or no traffic, and no other people are around. The shoot is casual – about a dozen of us are walking and talking in groups of three or four, and the photographer on the bicycle taking shots of us is Diana!

I wonder how she manages to ride the bike and take the photos at the same time, but she does so effortlessly – even though the wheels of her bike come very close to the kerb as she stops to take yet another shot.

During a short break, she grins at me and seems very excited. "Wouldn't it be great if we could get these pictures developed straight away," she says. I nod. "I wonder if our sponsors will pay for them to be developed rush-rush," I reply.

By far the most striking aspect of the shoot is her absolute informality. The whole thing is just like any bunch of people out having fun, anywhere. That's part of her genius, I think to myself as I watch her at work; and that's how she gets so much out of everyone she meets – they're too busy having fun to be overawed or any nonsense like that . . .

I wake up, and head for my PC to get this down. A little later, when I tell my friend Sheena, who is a film producer, about this dream, she says, "Diana wasn't talking about photos – she was telling us to get your screenplays into development straight away!"

Next day I visit my sister Audrey for lunch in the country and tell her about the dream. She says exactly the same as Sheena.

Thank you, ladies!

Although the rose has gone

O N THE FOURTH anniversary of Diana's departure, while walking along the Kensington Road, I noticed a small crowd gathered at the gates of Kensington Palace and decided to take a closer look.

Hundreds of bouquets, photographs, cards, sketches, poems, drawings, paintings and letters had been fixed to the gates, and to the railings on either side of them. The hand-written messages were all intensely personal and deeply felt. One or two, which spoke of the 'betrayal' of Diana, were couched in very strong language indeed. I couldn't help wondering if the tenants of the palace had seen them. If they had, they must have been deeply shocked and dismayed.

Among the many gentler ones, the following caught my eye:

Diana,
You meant the world to us, even though it's four years since you
left us. Your friends will never forget you. How could we? You
would be so proud of Wills and Harry, God bless them. They also
have your looks, which a lot of the group might not like. God
bless Diana, our sorrow. We never met. Till the day we do meet,
God bless always. So proud to call you Queen of Hearts.

From the Morgan family. X X
Stratford
London E15

Do not stand at my grave and weep.
I am not there, I do not sleep.
I am a thousand winds that blow
I am the diamond glints on snow.
I am the sunlight on ripened grain
I am the gentle autumn rain.
When you awaken in the morning's hush
I am the swift uplifting rush
of quiet birds in circled flight
I am the soft stars that shine at night.
Do not stand at my grave and cry
I am not there, I did not die.

Anon

Although the rose has gone,
the perfume still remains.

Mrs A Clark
Bucks

Word-play

I AWAKE AT 6 a.m. Something is telling me that there's an extraordinary anagram hiding in the title of the first section of this book – Diana's own description of where she is, and how she sees things from her new perspective.

I get out of bed, go to my desk, reach for a pen and paper and, a few moments later, there it is.

I smile, shake my head and look up at the sky outside. "You people really are outrageous," I say out loud.

Judge for yourself.

Rearrange the letters of *A Matter of Life And 'Death'*, and what do we get?

Draft me the tale of Diana.

PART 5

Apocalypse now

*You know, I feel the whole of humankind
is poised for a mass awakening.*

Antares
In an e-mail to the Earth Rainbow Network
August, 2001

At valley forge, George Washington had a rather special visitor. He later described her as "a beautiful female apparition". She showed him three dramatic scenes concerning the future of America. Finally she said:
"Son of the Republic, what you have seen is thus interpreted: three perils will come upon this Republic. The most fearful is the third, passing which, the whole world united shall never be able to prevail against her. Nor shall ever have reason to."

Later, Washington said, "With these words the figure vanished. I started from my seat, feeling that I had been shown the birth, progress and destiny of the Republic of the United States."

Anthony Sherman
The National Tribune
December, 1880

Apocalypse now

*The ultimate weakness of violence is that it is a
descending spiral, begetting the very thing it seeks to destroy.
Instead of diminishing evil, it multiplies it. Through violence
you may murder the liar, but you cannot murder the lie,
nor establish the truth. Through violence you may murder
the hater, but you do not murder hate. In fact, violence merely
increases hate. So it goes. Returning violence for violence
multiplies violence, adding deeper darkness to a night already
devoid of stars. Darkness cannot drive out darkness: only light
can do that. Hate cannot drive out hate: only love can do that.*

Martin Luther King, Jr.

An eye for an eye makes the whole world blind.

Mahatma Gandhi

IN THE DAYS that followed the cataclysm in New York, a blizzard
of e-mail swept round the world. It came in three distinct
flavours: Most of the messages expressed horror, grief and
outrage; a few examined the situation with a calm, almost
Olympian detachment, and dared to face the shocking truth that
all was not what it appeared to be: that the ultimate responsibility
for what had just happened did *not* lie where we were being told it
lay; the remainder dared to suggest that, despite all appearances to
the contrary, something wonderful could come of it all.

For several days I found myself wondering what Diana was
thinking; and as I awoke one morning, I had my answer:

MJ

Did September 11 and its aftermath hit you as hard as it hit all of us – particularly those who have lost loved ones?

Diana

Of course it did. We wept for everyone whose life on Earth had been shattered. We wept for their families and loved ones. We wept for those heroic fire-fighters, who gave their lives. We wept, not only for America but for the world.

What I am going to say now might seem strange – it might even seem tactless and inappropriate – but when we had dried our tears, we began to celebrate; and we are still celebrating.

Because September 11 was the flashpoint, the spark that ignited a huge explosion of quite another kind. I don't really need to tell *you* this, because you already know it, but here goes anyway:

September 11 was a wake-up call. It woke almost the entire human race, except those still fast asleep (and by that, I don't mean in bed).

It smashed many of the barriers we have built up between us, and revealed that we're all in the same boat now.

It also revealed that, because of the weapons we've created in recent years, it no longer makes sense to fight any more, because if we do, *everyone* is going to lose: the ship'll go down with all of us aboard – *Titanic* on a global scale. And that simply cannot happen. Correction – it won't be allowed:

I am told that if anyone presses the Armageddon button now, the reverse of what we all dread is going to occur. I don't know what that means exactly – nobody does – but I certainly hope and pray it's true.

Whenever light grows brighter, the surrounding shadow seems to get darker. So, focus on the light; increase the light; *become* the light . . .

We all send you our love and thoughts and prayers. We ask you to do the same for each other. And if you've got a few left over, please send them in our direction too – there's a lot going on up here at the moment, as some of you know, and any help we can get will be more than welcome, I can assure you.

Postscript, May 2003:

MJ
Is there *never* to be an end to hostility and war on Earth?

Diana
If there *has* to be another war, let it not be against human beings, let it be against ignorance, fear, violence, selfishness, secrecy and greed. Let the leaders of the nations have the courage to put it to their peoples. Let the human race speak, for the first time in history. Let there be a world Referendum:

Which is it to be? Endless war – or endless peace?

Prepare yourselves for a terrible shock, gentlemen: there will be a landslide vote for endless peace.

What conclusion can we draw from this? That throughout history, it has suited certain individuals, for reasons of their own, to keep the nations at each other's throats.

For thousands of years they have presided over the slaughter. It is still going on today: Past mistakes and past crimes have always been used as an excuse for launching still more horror, and the sacrifice of still more innocents – those poor, conditioned fighting men and women who are trained to fight to kill.

The war in Iraq was *not* a holy war, whatever you might have been told. There's no such thing as a holy war! Killing one another, for whatever reason, is anything but holy.

If I had the power to stop the war machine in its tracks, all over the world; to immobilise it once and for all and send all opposing armies home to their families, I wouldn't hesitate for a moment. But I have an even better idea:

You stop it! You, the people, have the right to announce to the whole world: "War is no longer an acceptable means of resolving our differences. Let us now devise other ways of resolving them."

Invite *everyone* to vote on this motion. What are you waiting for?!

And to signal your long-awaited victory when it comes — and come it will — may Light explode all round the Earth, like the biggest fireworks display of all time, filling the hearts and minds of everyone alive.

May a moment of indescribable joy and love and revelation hit the Earth like an asteroid — *now*! And if not now — soon!

May the nightmare end, and may the party begin. There, I have said it. Happy?!

MJ

Thank you, Diana. I think you know how ready most of us are for that party . . .

A new Heaven and a new Earth

The greatest secret ever kept is the identity of man.
We are powerful, creator Gods who have come from every
comer of the galaxy to be on Earth at this crucial time,
when mankind and the Earth are ascending
into a new energetic frequency . . .

Almine
A Life of Miracles

HERE ARE JUST a few of the memorable e-mails I received in the wake of the World Trade Centre disaster in New York:

This could be the turning point in human history, the point at which we release the need to hate each other, to seek revenge for one crime after another, to kill others in the name of faith, reason and justice.

There is in this moment another golden opportunity. With those clouds of dust and smoke emerged the priceless potential for the nations truly to know each other at last, regardless of colour, creed, faith, country, beliefs.

From the rubble can arise the new human race, linked heart to heart, soul to soul, spirit to spirit as we finally recognise that this is our time to come forth and *be* the new – the phoenix from the ashes, humanity at its finest.

Soleira Green
Soleira@SOULutions.co.uk
14 September 2001

Friends and Family, I have witnessed the fulfilment of prophecy, the opening of the gateway to the next world, the Fifth World of Peace, and I have seen the Guardians of the Gate that pose the questions, the challenges we must rise to meet. Ask these questions of yourself now, as they will surely be asked by the Guardians over the next five years:

Why are we here?
Where did we come from?
Who are we?
What must we release, in order to be
all that we came here to be?

Maria Yraceburu
earthwisdom@earthlink.net
21 September 2001

The Day of Truth –
Kiara Windrider

As I was meditating this morning, I linked with Babaji, the planetary avatar, in a superconscious state, to ask him whether he had any insights into what was going on these days. His response follows:

Dear ones, you are at the threshold of a planetary birth. Old forms are dissolving; new forms are arising. You have been conditioned on this planet to believe that birth is something painful, and so it is for you. Even so, the moment of your birth has arrived, and will be truly a wondrous, sacred event.

You are aware of the convergence of many cycles of time, prophesied through ancient calendars and scriptures all over the world. Just as a mother knows when her time is coming, and her labour begins, so is Mother Earth now pushing to birth a new consciousness, a new Age.

Would it help you to know that, difficult as these times may seem to you, the promised new Age will surely come? There are those locked in duality who would seek to prevent this, and there will be for a time a great struggle of increased polarisation.

This is all in divine order. Please know that the Brotherhoods of Light have long prepared for this time as well. In the times ahead, no longer will it be possible for anyone to sit on the fences of indifference, apathy or denial.

A planetary wake-up call has been issued. The last trumpet has been sounded. As hearts and souls awaken, cries of freedom will grow from within, and the bands of fear that have enslaved humanity for long eons will be lifted. As the bands of fear are released, a new Earth will be born.

The Kingdom of God has always been with you and among you, and now will be revealed through the waves of light, love and freedom that sweep through the planet in this moment of birth.

Many of you are asking, what do these recent events of September 11 mean? Are we heading towards a global war? Is the world about to end? Please realise that the discordant energies that fuelled the events of this day have been brewing for quite some time. Billions have already suffered around the world in a war on the human spirit. This will only end as deeper truth is brought to light. And so it shall be.

You might be aware of the symbolic calendar coded into the measurements of the Great Pyramid, ending on September 17, 2001 at the doorway of the King's Chamber, the chamber of initiation.

Just as the life of a caterpillar ends only so that it may cocoon into a butterfly, so as you stand at this threshold of initiation, a great portal of light opens before you.

Life on this planet will never again be the same. The events of September 11 are directly linked to these calendar measurements, signifying a planetary initiation the like of which has not been witnessed in recent ages.

The Hopis called this the Day of Purification. We are calling it the Day of Truth. This is indeed a wondrous time, a time for light to shine into all the dark places of the human heart, so that all that was hidden may now be revealed and transmuted in the great cauldron of humanity's awakening.

Hold this vision strong. Do not give in to despair and polarity consciousness, no matter what the appearances may be. When waves of fear, dread or anger come up, transmute them in violet flame. Continue calling on the realms of light for assistance. Trust the process.

If you could see these times from the perspective of the Age that follows, you would truly be dancing in the streets in profound gratitude for the openings that lie before you.

The time for a planetary re-birth is at hand!

Kiara Windrider
Wind.rider@eudoramail.com, Fall Equinox, 2001

Greater love hath no man than this

FIREFIGHTER CHRISTIAN WAUGH, 55, helped to carry the body of Father Mychal Judge, the Fire Department chaplain, out from Tower One of the World Trade Centre:

> Father Judge was standing about 20ft away from us in the lobby, and when the second plane hit, the debris from the second building came down and blew into the lobby of Tower One. The dust and the wind blew us over, and everything went jet black. As it started to lift, I found Father Judge lying there. I think he died of a heart attack. We put him in a chair and carried him out.
>
> His nephew says if it wasn't for Father Judge, the five of us would have been trapped. So he got us out of the building by dying.

Dee O'Connell
The Observer Magazine
London, 17 February 2002

Mother Mary speaks

"**D**O NOT MOURN those who have left, for they have come home into my heart, into the house of many mansions and many rooms of my Son. They now walk in the garden with the Father. They have ascended and now wear the robes of Ascension, as they gave themselves as the sacrificial lambs in the slaughterhouse of the now.

"Know, my dear ones, that they will again come forth into and onto your world. They rest not long on their laurels in the Light. They come forth again – genuinely happy to assist – with full memory, full light, and full knowledge for the future."

Gabbitas1@aol.com
Tuesday, 2 October 2001

I was destined to be there that day. I think God was with me, guiding my every step, taking me there and taking me out. Our life is made up of inches and seconds and steps, and had one of those steps been different, I could have been killed. And now I think there must have been a reason I wasn't.

Ed Fine
A New Jersey businessman who was visiting the World Trade Centre on 11 September 2001, and led a group of office workers to safety from the 78th floor.

Heroes of Ground Zero

Dee O'Connell
The Observer Magazine,
London, 17 February 2002

Year of Manifestation

WE ARE NOW in the midst of transition. As always happens before there is a birth, there is labor. The birth of the Fifth World of Peace means transition and effort. As the Fifth World comes there will be 'growing pains'.

But there has been planted in our world a seed that is growing, and the efforts to nurture the seed have been successful. The prophecies have foretold of this time. It is happening even now.

There are many big changes happening. There have been breakups, and there have been upheavals. There is what many consider darkness and difficulty. Many say, "Things are getting worse." But, there is behind all this a power which is making for the evolution of the world.

Many of us have seen, or are now seeing, the world as it shall be. That vision we try to convey to those who are receptive, to inspire them to go on with their work. The images I have been shown tell me it is now only a matter of time.

As the Children of the Four Directions come together, we recognise that all politics, religion, science and knowledge are part of one thing. As we heal and embrace our true identity as responsible co-creators, pain, sorrow, fear, mourning and unhappiness are dissipating and our world moves to become a place of smiles and happy laughter. The greatest teacher in our world today is one who can work to lift the sorrows of others and make the lives of others better.

In the old, Fourth World, which is now passing, when one individual had something, instead of using it to help others, he tried to keep it for himself, with the result that in time a system developed that is now collapsing because its foundations were out of balance with the whole.

But as people begin to develop their God-given gifts and use them for the benefit of All, we are building on an unshakable foundation, one that is rooted in love, and therefore indestructible.

These are not new things that I am telling you. They are the old, old truths that have been taught for many, many centuries, and are now re-emerging at this crucial planetary moment.

The sacred Law is springing into effect; the light of Spirit is penetrating the darkness, and out of chaos and disorder there is being built the Fifth World of Peace, where there is *no* inequality, *no* injustice, *no* division between those who have too much and those who have too little; where all gifts will be divided and all the bounty will be evenly shared.

Maria Yraceburu
earthwisdom@earthlink.net
26 November 2001

Solara's Surf Report for the Year 2002: Leaping Over The Gap

When the world as we know it shatters,
when we have nowhere to go, except into the unknown,
then we will either be given something new to stand on
or we will be taught how to fly!

Parallel Realities

ON SEPTEMBER 11, 2001 we collectively experienced what is known as "the shattering of all known worlds". The world as we knew it null-zoned and ceased to exist. In an instant, our priorities were completely rearranged. Many of the veils suddenly dissolved and numerous illusions shattered, leaving us in a place that was new and unknown. We had left the old map and entered uncharted territory . . .

For many, this was a moment of great awakening. We had been thrust out of our old world. It had simply collapsed in upon itself and no longer existed. It wasn't at all comfortable to be so vulnerable and open – we realised that we had to become more real and honest than ever before in order to inhabit this greater reality – we must be prepared to move our beings and our lives onto a much vaster scale.

2002 will be a year of immense breakthroughs. It will be a year in which our creative expression will overflow the blockages which have been in place for several years. The lights will finally turn green and we will be able to move forward as never before.

We have already entered the first outer set of gates and are now in the passageway that leads to the inner gates.

The passage through this vestibule is sacred. We know that we are going through the inner gates into a new way of being. And we can already feel that, once we go through the inner gates, our lives will be irrevocably changed.

Happy New Year!

Ride with the wind!

Solara
01.01.2002
Starborne Unlimited
6426 Hwy.935.#6511
Whitefish, Montana 59937

A dream

D-day, 6 June, 2002

IN THE SMALL HOURS I have a dream. So real that it wakes me: I am in a small courtyard, outside a house, sitting opposite Diana and one of her friends (I'm not sure if it is a young man or a young woman). We are using a pack of cards to do some divination. Diana has first go: she closes her eyes, shuffles the pack, pulls out one card and turns it over:

The Ace of Hearts.

"The Grail," I announce, feeling rather excited.

Her friend hands me the pack.

"We usually do a three-card reading," I say, before shuffling. I close my eyes, concentrate for a moment or two, select three cards from different places in the pack, and turn them over.

The first two are the Queen of Hearts and the Knave of Hearts.

"That's us," I say to Diana, my heart pounding.

The third card is the Ace of Hearts.

Diana comes round the table and sits down, so close that her right hip touches my left. I put my arm round her waist. Her midriff is bare, and I gently stroke it as we continue to talk . . .

Then I wake up.

A conversation in the night

2 July, 2002

THE TENSION AND excitement are building up. Diana and I and various friends are sitting outside the house at a garden table, discussing the next moves. The first copy of this book arrives. I look at the cover, smile, then grow serious, realising that this is it – the moment I have been postponing since the very beginning of this project: The unaskable question has to be asked. *Now.*

MJ

Diana, one of the first things you said was, "There are planetary databanks up here. Everything that has ever happened on Earth is recorded in hologram form." So the question everyone wants answered is: "Was your death an accident? And if not, who was responsible?"

There is a long silence. I try again:

MJ

If that question isn't answered, surely the credibility of this book is going to be seriously undermined.

Another silence follows. Diana takes a deep breath, then lets it out.

Diana

Yes, there *are* records up here. And yes, everything that happens on Earth *is* recorded. As you know, many deaths are accidental, and many are not. Mine was not. It was planned before I was born – with my full consent and approval, and that of everyone else involved.

And when the time came, everything conspired to bring the cast and the stage together, in order for it to play itself out. There is no blame here, no need for any recrimination whatsoever.

I can feel her relief, now that she has finally taken the plunge. Unexpectedly, Diana smiles.

> Diana (contd)
> There's no death, so what's the point of trying to kill anyone?

She exchanges a glance with her friends, and one or two of them nod almost imperceptibly.

> Diana (contd)
> My death was no more important than anyone else's. But I am told that it served the purpose it was designed for, and for that I am more grateful than I could ever express in words.

I nod. Apparently, during the week following her death, the grief and love being felt by a third of the population of the world was seen on the inner planes as the opening of a gigantic, pink-and-white lotus flower, representing the heart chakra. Rarely, if ever, had the lotus been opened so fully in so many human beings at the same time, I was told. And its fragrance is with us still – in the determination of most people on Earth that soon, another way must be found for conducting human affairs.

In other words, the long age of hatred, distrust and hostility between nations and creeds and cultures is about to be replaced by something else altogether. Something so simple that it has been totally overlooked – the Prime Directive itself, no less, which we buried or mislaid thousands of years ago:

"Love one another."

A parting gift

UNTIL WE MEET AGAIN – which won't be too long now, I hope – I'd like to leave you with this thought:

We are *all* heroes; we've *all* struggled on and on, not knowing who we really are, where we came from, or what we are supposed to be doing now that we're here. But not for much longer.

Life is meant to be a journey of discovery, a 'magical mystery tour' – *not* an endless horror film in which we are all trapped.

There *are* no enemies 'out there' – that's an illusion kept alive by those who, for reasons of their own, want us to remain trapped in the nightmare.

But everything changes. We're gradually waking up, which means that the nightmare is almost over. Having gone through the fire, we'll soon be rising above it like the phoenix, and soaring above the battlefield where we've been fighting all these years.

You might not think so, watching the news unfold each day, but we *are* going to win. We *are* going to survive. We *are* going to reach our goal. We *are* going to fulfill our destiny.

A message for Michael

O N THE VERY DAY I 'closed' the third or fourth draft of this book — September, 2002 — my good friend Margaret More was about to e-mail me when Diana herself drew near and said, "I have a message for Michael too. May I go first?!"

Margaret, who knows Diana of old, said, "Of course," — and the result, which she enclosed with her own message, is below. Needless to say, it totally blew me away, as it seemed to confirm that Diana herself is happy with the book, and deems it finished. Judge for yourself:

My dear friend,
Allow me to speak to you through my friend and former companion Margaret, as she is known now. We worked together in the eons of time to repair the rifts in the tapestry torn down by the intransigence of mankind. Not only men, you understand . . .

This is how we came to be in contact with you at this time — another of the fellow workers in the Universe of lighting the lamps of Peace — come to you now in the presence of Our Maker to rejoice in the communication I have with you. A communication so profound that sometimes I marvel at that which we're allowed to do.

I must go now. Rely on me to be at your beck and call MOST of the time!

Yours in Light and the Love of the Universe of One,

Diana

You probably noticed that the wording of the above is rather more formal than usual. I think that's because Margaret was using her own wording, which is more formal than Diana's, when she recorded the incoming message . . .

Love to Diana (i)

Hundreds of cards and bouquets were pinned to the gates of Kensington Palace in September, 2002, the fifth anniversary of Diana's funeral. They included the following:

"Siempre serás la Reina de Inglaterra."
Ma Carmen

"No other Royal can give that
spontaneous love! You touched the heart
of millions of people, and today
we remember you."

Love,
Lydia
XXX

"Imagine that wonderful moment when
Holly and Jessica met Princess Diana –
a stoop, that smile, such love . . .
and a blinding light."

Hue

"No matter what people say,
you're still missed, and so many still love you
and will never forget you."

Love,
Maureen

Diana, who effortlessly captured
and endeared the world like no other.
Those who tried to cage her spirit
didn't understand that her soul had no limit.
She has blessed the world forever.

Amanda Abel
Florida, USA

ROYALS – TAKE NOTE:
WE WILL NEVER FORGET DIANA

Dear Prince William and Prince Harry,
Just to reassure you that there is a tremendous
groundswell of love and respect for your precious
mother in our island home and beyond our shores.
Your mother's unique contribution to life on Earth
during the 20th century has yet to be accorded
its rightful place in history.

Mary Ratcliffe
Swindon, Wiltshire

"And she shall make the face of heaven so bright
that all the world will be in love with night."

Anonymous
(*Adapted from* Romeo and Juliet, *III. i.*
by William Shakespeare)

A dream

Sunday, 27 October, 2002 at 04.44a.m.

D IANA AND I ARE standing in a small office, conferring over papers and diagrams. She is wearing a white silk shirt, chinos, flat heels, a single row of pearls.

"On the day of days," I say to her, "you must look exquisite."

"On the day of days, I must look as if I know what I'm doing," she replies.

Yeah, sure, I think to myself, that goes without saying. "You must look exquisite," I repeat.

She smiles. "That can be arranged," she says, then looks at me. "And you will be there, my friend." She lifts my hand to her lips and kisses it.

I am blown away by this loving, courtly gesture – the reverse of the customary man-kisses-woman's-hand – which I recognise from somewhere.

I wake, turn on the light, reach for pen and paper.

An explosion of Light

David Cousins
September, 1997

DIANA STOOD BEHIND each person as they said their piece. When her brother began to deliver his passionate speech, the black rose he came in with crumbled – especially as he became emotional towards the end – and energy rushed up from his lower centres to form a white rose in his heart.

While this was happening, an impulse from the cosmic Christ moved through Hyde Park and people responded with heart and soul – they started to applaud, and the clapping grew in intensity and gathered speed, just like those 'Mexican waves' created by spectators on the terraces of football stadiums.

The Abbey stands at the intersection of a number of ley lines, and as the applause in Hyde Park and Whitehall was taken up, first by the crowd outside the Abbey, and then by the congregation inside, a huge explosion of light raced down the ley lines throughout Britain and into all the other countries that are connected to those leys.

As the sound of the applause rolled down the aisle towards the coffin, I noticed that the higher aspect of Diana was holding a pile of golden powder, like fairy dust. She blew one single kiss into it, which sent out millions of sparks of white light into everyone on Earth who is part of the network of Light.

These sparks also went out to the Royal family and everyone connected with Diana – not just those who had at some time been in her physical presence and those who had lined the roads of the funeral procession, but to everyone who had visited one of the temporary shrines where flowers had been laid, and also to all those linked to her via radio and television.

As this 'one final kiss' – this symbol of humility, symbol of love – went out around the planet, these tiny specks of white light began to coalesce within the planet itself, creating a gigantic roselike structure that is going to grow and grow until it permeates all life forms. My impression is that this vibration will continue to grow for the next five years – almost as if a thought-form has now been wrapped round the planet which will create a rotation of its own.

During this period it will allow a much greater rapport, telepathically and otherwise. In this way the necessary adjustments can be made, especially in governmental agencies, in political and religious groups; in fact, everywhere where essential change has to take place.

It is almost as if that one kiss has melted the opposition that was and will be, so that the new 'doorway' can now be simply opened. With that one kiss, a lot of dark doorways all over the world slammed shut, howls of protest from the dark agencies faded into silence, and then a number of new doorways were opened in the Himalayas, in certain parts of Mexico and on the ocean bed.

That one kiss opened not only the hearts and minds of countless people on Earth, but also awoke life that had been latent, elsewhere in the Solar system. The crystal skulls were also lit up, as were all the crystals that constitute the subtle anatomy of the physical world. In other words, the crystals paid their own homage in whatever way was necessary.

While Elton John sang *Candle in the Wind*, Diana stood behind him, her hand resting lightly on his shoulder, and swayed in time to the music. Elton John was also momentarily overshadowed by the cosmic Christ, which suffused his voice and music, and in doing so touched many millions of people.

The pathway home

When Diana gave her *Panorama* interview, she was sowing the seed of the idea of 'Queen of Hearts', preparing mankind to link into her through the heart. And when she later gave away a lot of her wardrobe for the charity auction, she was on one level preparing for her departure.

Throughout the week that preceded the funeral, a third of the population of the world was grieving for all that they had lost. But on the day itself, we were all given the opportunity to release that loss and grief, and to prepare for the rebirth, or resurrection, which was taking place.

When the service ended and the coffin was escorted out of the cathedral, Diana did not follow, as a white-gold pathway opened up, about 30 to 40 metres wide, and she shot straight up like a rocket, into the light, the golden road, the pathway of the Golden Thread which is followed by those who have earned the right to bring the Divine Light of the Father's purpose into physical matter.

On either side of the path, her friends and family on the inner planes who were waiting for her grand exit, were all applauding because they recognised the importance of what she had done. They were all grinning hugely at a superb performance, and at the release of a soul returning to the hearts and minds of those who had missed her greatly.

Diana's mission

"THE ENERGIES THAT were set in motion at the time of Diana's passing are still rippling out through the Universes, continuing to touch a great multitude of beings in ways, times and places of which we know not.

"Once sent forth, energies cannot be called back, but continue on their outward-bound journeys and become, in a sense, missions on their own. Thus, Diana's mission lives on in the energetic message emitted in 1997 which is travelling on, much as a comet moves through the cosmos."

Saint Germain
A message received by Carolyn J Holtgrewe in August, 2002,
on the fifth anniversary of Diana's departure.

The full texts of the messages delivered by Saint Germain in 1997 and 1998 can be read at the Galactic Foundation's web site:
http://www.galacticfoundation.com

Thank you!

ALMA, AVA, ORSON, WSC, Saint Germain, Maria Kazan, Sidney, Elsie, Lillian, Len, Maureen, AB, AR, AE, WTP, Kaye, H-A, Ellen Easton, Tom, Zoë and Ted, MJ, LJ, JJ, PJ, AJ, AN, AW, River, Justin . . .

Peter Quiller and Simon Peter Fuller, whose unfailing guidance and encouragement made this book possible; Petey, whose editorial skill painlessly reduced it from lumbering heavyweight to manageable middleweight; and James, for being the best brother anyone ever had.

Very special thanks to Audrey, Chris, Nicolette, RO'R & Catherine, Merryn, Julian, Glenna, Moira & Mahin, Dave & Colette, Simon Dee, Fran & Julie, Aish Jeneby, Molly Daubeny, Ann, Robert & Philip Donaldson, Silver, Layla, the divine Julie & Patrick, Bran, Mandy, Lucy, Damian, Tim, John Prudhoe, Bob & Donna, Kevin & Caroline, Gwynneth, Terry Kane, Peter Carbines, Richard Elen, Jerry Simer, Karen, Michelle Stutts, Jacqueline Stallone, Aldo, Mark, Noël, Will, Rosanna, Gita, Jennifer, Heather & William, Richard Heritage, Johnnie Walker & Tiggy, Eleanor, David Gray, Hazel Courteney, Suzie, Nesta Wyn Ellis, Laura, Jo Berry, Timothy, Ocean, Elijah, Noah Pollaczek. To Irene, for her prayers. To Sarah, for her vision. Mia Christou, for her courage.

To Bonita Corso, Jan Goldstoff, Meredith Bernstein, Krystyna Spicer and 'the Women of Vision' in New York – and all the soul brothers and sisters in Los Angeles.

Vera Stanley Alder The Initiation of the World (*Rider*)
Ken Carey Starseed: The Third Millennium
(*HarperCollins*)

Helena Paterson   The Celtic Tarot (*Aquarian Press*)
Ariel Spillsbury   The Mayan Oracle: Return Path to the
Stars
& Michael Bryner   (*Bear & Co, Santa Fe, NM*)

. . . and also to Bryan Appleyard, James Benson, Julie Burchill, Hillary Rodham Clinton, David Cousins, Peter Dawkins, David Dimbleby, M. Valéry Giscard d'Estaing, John Ezard, Anthony Holden, Carolyn Holtgrewe, Christopher Hudson, Christina Lamb, Nigella Lawson, Alan Masters, Peter McKay, Michael O'Mara, Petey, Peter Quiller, William Rees-Mogg, Andrew Sullivan, Sharon Whiteman – for shedding light on the phenomenal events surrounding the life and work and legend of Diana, Queen of Hearts. To Rosie Boycott, for her portrait of Diana as a 20th century Cinderella.

And to Matthew Smith, for welcoming this book with open arms, an open mind and an open heart . . .

To the Earl Spencer, for kindly allowing me to reproduce his memorable tribute to his sister. To Jean Hudon, a good friend and ally in Canada, for his vital contribution to **The Human Family**. To Suzy and Matthew Ward, Eleanor Lister, Mavis Meaker and Margaret More, bridge-builders between the worlds . . .

To Yve Betar, for your wonderful *Reflections on the Goddess*; to Arthur Miller, for confirming that a writer *should* listen when those inner voices speak; to Mr Kofi Annan, Secretary-General of the United Nations, and Lord Rothermere, chairman of Associated Newspapers in London, for their open minds and their generosity of spirit . . .

To Soleira Green, Maria Yraceburu, Solara and Kiara Windrider, for revealing that out of the smoke and rubble of 11 September, 2001, something wonderful was already beginning to emerge . . .

To Bob Silverstein, a knight in silver armour, who suddenly appeared when all seemed lost. To David Furnish and Elton John, for their kind permission to use *Goodbye, England's* Rose as a chapter heading. And to Oprah Winfrey, Spirit's very own standard-bearer . . .

To Tony, for triggering the extraordinary adventure that is still in progress – and for providing the all-weather compass that has kept us on track . . .

To the invisible army of Lightworkers, all round the planet . . .

To the Lady; to the Father; to the King; to the Master of Ceremonies; to Merlin, a much-loved teacher and friend during this lifetime and, I suspect, others; to the Commander-in-Chief – the Archangel Michael; to our mother, Earth, and all the Nature kingdoms. And, finally, to all our 'friends in high places' – our guardian angels – for everything they do for us all, unseen and, far too often, unacknowledged . . .

Travelling companions

Here are just a few of the memorable books that have kept me company on my travels and adventures, made me think, inspired me to soldier on in every kind of weather:

(* = out of print)	Author	Publisher
The Avatars*	'A E'	Macmillan
The Candle of Vision*	'A.E.'	Macmillan
The Initiation Of The World	Vera Stanley Alder	Rider
The Shining Paths	DoloresAshcroft-Nowicki	Aquarian Press
Life In The World Unseen*	Anthony Borgia	Corgi
The Mists Of Avalon	Marion Bradley	Michael Joseph
The Gods Of Eden	William Bramley	Avon
A Search In Secret Egypt	Paul Brunton	Rider
The Starseed Transmissions	Ken Carey	HarperCollins
Regents Of The Seven Spheres*	H K Challoner	TPH
The Wheel Of Rebirth*	H K Challoner	TPH
The Pendragon	Catherine Christian	Macmillan

Childhood's End	Arthur C Clarke	*Pan*
The Light In Britain	Grace & Ivan Cooke	*White Eagle*
Sun-Men Of The Americas	Grace & Ivan Cooke	*White Eagle*
Embraced By The Light	Betty Eadie	*Bantam*
Critical Path	R Buckminster Fuller	*St Martin's Press*
Rising Out Of Chaos	Simon Peter Fuller	*Kima Global*
Genesis of the Grail Kings	Laurence Gardner	*Bantam*
Initiation	Elisabeth Haich	*Allen & Unwin*
Dune	Frank Herbert	*NEL*
The Pendragon Cycle	Stephen R Lawhead	*Avon*
The Awakening Letters	Rosamond Lehmann	*Spearman*
Our Son Moves Among You *	Mary Long	*Bachman Turner*
ET 101: Cosmic Instruction Manual		Diana Luppi
Intergalactic		
Bringers Of The Dawn	Barbara Marciniak	*Bear & Co.*
The View Over Atlantis	John Michell	*Abacus*
Ultimate Journey	Robert Monroe	*Doubleday*
Life After Life	Raymond A Moody	*Bantam*
A Handbook Of Angels	HC Moolenburgh	*Daniel*
The Healing Secret of the Ages	Catherine Ponder	*A Thomas & Co*
Merlin Awakens	Peter Quiller	*Firebird*
Quest for the Round Table	Peter Quiller	*Dragonfly*
The Celestine Prophecy	James Redfield	*WarnerBantam*
Seth Speaks	Jane Roberts	*Prentice Hall*
The 12th Planet	Zecharia Sitchin	*Avon*
The Wind Of Change	Julie Soskin	*Barton House*
Links With Space	David Spangler	*Findhorn Press*
The Death of Merlin*	Walter Johannes Stein	*Floris*
The Crystal Cave	Mary Stewart	*Coronet*
The Hollow Hills	Mary Stewart	*Coronet*
The Holographic Universe	Michael Talbot	*HarperPerennial*
Powershift	Alvin Toffler	*Pan*
The Third Wave	Alvin Toffler	*Pan*
Shambhala, Oasis Of Light *	Andrew Tomas	*Sphere*

Highlands Of Heaven	Rev. Vale Owen	*Greater World*
Matthew, tell me about Heaven	Suzanne Ward	*Matthew Books*
The Book of Merlyn	T H White	*Univ. of Texas*
The Once And Future King	T H White	*Fontana*
Autobiography Of A Yogi	Paramhamsa Yogananda	*Rider*
The Wild Swans	Yung Chang	*HarperCollins*

Cover

Portrait of Diana by Kim Knott / Camera Press.

*The authors of this book have dedicated
all their royalties to the education project*

*whose purpose is to empower young people
to make the most of their lives, and to
prepare to inherit the Earth.*

"It's up to **us** now . . ."

Acknowledgments

Although it is not the general custom to seek formal permission to reproduce e-mail or briefly to quote the published work of other writers, provided that one acknowledges those writers and, where applicable, their publishers, I am most grateful to the many authors whom I have briefly quoted in this book, and acknowledged.

As for the longer quotes, I have made every effort to contact the authors or their publishers, and have not always received a reply. If the author and publisher of any long quotation in *Love from Diana* wish me to acknowledge their permission in future editions of this book, I shall be most grateful if they will contact me via my publishers.

I would also like to thank the members of the public whose memorable tributes to Diana I have quoted in the *Coronation* section of this book. There were no addresses on the cards and letters carrying these tributes outside the royal palaces and elsewhere.

Michael Joseph

Also by Michael Joseph

Cane! (with Robert Donaldson) Sphere
(made into the 6-part TV series *Fields of Fire*) Zenith Films
Wilderness (with Robert Donaldson) Hamish Hamilton
The Guide Book (with Tony Neate) Gateway
Merlin the Immortal (with Peter Quiller) Spirit of Celtia
Angels: Close Encounters of Another Kind (in preparation)
Legends: The Hollywood Immortals (profiles)
Earthrise: A Journey to the End of Time (in preparation)
The Dragon King:
1. *A Prince among Men*
2. *The Seeding of the Light* (in preparation)

(e)motion pictures for the Millennium
The Dragon King:
1. *A Prince among Men*
2. *The Seeding of the Light* (in preparation)
A Princess in New York
On the Other Side of the Sky: Adventures in the Afterlife
Mr Universe: Misadventures in the Afterlife
Mission: Earth (with Peter Carbines)
Catch the Lightning
Battle Royal (with Peter Quiller, in preparation)
Out of Time (with Peter Carbines, in preparation)

Novelisation
On the Other Side of the Sky: Adventures in the Afterlife
Mr Universe: Misadventures in the Afterlife
Mission: Earth

Education
US I Winning the Life Game . . .
US II Running the Race of Our Lives . . .
US III Letting the Magic Happen . . .

Young people are about to become the *first* subject in their own education.

223

Diana's 'death'. And now her book. Two earthquakes of biblical proportions, shaking the entire planet to the core. What do you suppose they will, or already have, registered on the Richter scale? At least an 8 or 9.

And what will follow to surpass them in intensity – to wake anyone still asleep? Whatever it takes, I guess.

The ratcheting up process has begun in earnest now, with Diana adding her considerable power, and with so many others waiting 'on the other side'.

The balance is going to tip big time, and very soon. How can anyone not feel it?!

Maralee Gibson
New York

Thank you for the book – it's quite simply the greatest gift I've ever gotten in my life. I went away to Colorado to re-read it in peace and silence. You might not realise it, but believe me, this work is already beyond the seed stage – it's already well under way and heading for its fullest flower . . .

Shirley McGinnis
Phoenix, Arizona

As if they hadn't already stolen enough from us, now they're desperately trying to airbrush Diana out of history, sweep her under the carpet, pretend she never existed. Well I'm sorry, but she does exist – not only in the records of the twentieth century, but also in her sons, and in the hearts and minds and memories of countless millions of admirers around the world.

This wonderful book confirms that she has simply gone home – as we all do, when our time comes. Gone home to the higher dimension we all came from – of which the physical Universe is only a crude carbon copy . . .

Neil Sutherland
London

Love from Diana is a beautiful book that sings the praises of this fairy-tale princess who died too young yet left a legacy that will live through the ages.

Her tragic death touched the hearts of more people on this planet than anyone in history, and the lessons she imparts in this keepsake book will thrill her millions of ardent admirers around the world.

Bob Silverstein
Quicksilver Books
New York

At last . . . the message which the West has long awaited, confirming once more all that was made clear, centuries ago, to those who were ready to listen, to hear, to see, to believe – indeed, to know.

Thank God for God's patience and undying love.

Wonderful stuff!

Mahin Jung
London

Love to Diana (ii)

Hundreds more cards and bouquets were pinned to the gates of Kensington Palace in September, 2003, the sixth anniversary of Diana's funeral. They included the following:

Sunrise

You came up in glory
like sunrise over the world, to dazzle and turn it to gold,
to animate life on this Earth with your fresh light!

Your warm and glowing soul brought us a special joy,
made us laugh with happiness, but the force of your charm,
centred in your huge sparkling eyes,
reflected the flame of your love,
so keen to fulfil our wishes and dreams!

Most of all, your radiant smile
was like the rising sun, set to light up our path,
to give us power to get on with life,
optimism, and faith in brighter days to come!

Diana, Queen of Hearts,
simply, life with you was bliss:
You brought us not only delight but inner peace,
for you were that sunrise that set the world alight,
inspired us to march forward, to reach out
beyond the confines of the Earth,
to explore the Universe
and never go out, to blaze for eternity,
millennium after millennium!

Lucy
31 August, 2003

All peoples gazed at that goddess
with worship in their eyes, revered her.
Her godly message for today
was the only one they could trust.

Noble Diana, Queen of Hearts,
had a divine mission to show this cynical,
uncertain world that perfect love is the only way;
that the future of this world lies
within our own hearts . . .

Anon

She needed no royal title
to be our Queen:
She conquered the world
with the compassion in her heart,
more precious to those who loved her
than any Crown jewel.

Anon

Why did you go?
If only you would come back.
We need you so much,
We miss you so much.

adelina taddei
anna, porzia, gudran

Britain has lost
the biggest diamond in its Crown.

Anon

Missing Diana.

Prince Feel
South Korea

If love could build a stairway
and memories build a lane,
I'd climb straight up to heaven
and bring you back again.

Alan Tompsett
Chatham, Kent

I hope you're looking down at me
and watching over me, just as
I know you're watching over your sons.
I will never forget you, Diana.

Love,
Ashley
USA

For as long as history is recorded in Britain,
Diana, Princess of Wales will remain
the best loved and most sadly missed
of all the royals.

Anon